AF576429

THE BOND STORE TALES

THE BOND STORE TALES

Ross Gibson

A Museum of Sydney *on the site of first Government House* publication

Historic Houses Trust of New South Wales
Lyndhurst
61 Darghan St Glebe 2037

Published Sydney 1996

ISBN 0 949753 61 0

Museum of Sydney *on the site of first Government House*
is a property of the Historic Houses Trust of NSW

Cover image: ***Shipwreck, Kent*** (detail), artist unknown, c1890. National Library of Australia

FOREWORD

The Bond Store is the story-telling place in the Museum of Sydney. But these Pacific trading tales are about a moral economy not a cash nexus. For when material objects are traded between people the things that count are the intangible exchanges, of love, pride, honour, avarice, guilt or shame. These things endure.

These are travelling stories really; journeys through an oceanic world of water, dreams and blood; reflections and reveries, of blood ties and bloodshed; of chance meetings of strangers and strange events that end in new ways of thinking and feeling. Water and dreams always work their magic. They float the flotsam and jetsam of all our oceanic imaginings, of our own pasts and futures, fragments of memory, deliriums of desire, so many frail attempts to make sense of ourselves, to make us flow into each other, into sense of place, into history.

Sailors have always known this. Ross Gibson's mariner tales of Sydney's Pacific waterworld have liberated that wisdom from the seaman's chest, and in so doing liberated the museum from its bond to the plunderers of the past, and to the relic specialists of the present. By allowing others to tell their tales, by listening, each to the other, we make new bonds that acknowledge difference, exchange customs, pay our dues to self and society, to each other. Surely this is the moral economy of the operations of Pacific trade, the cultural riches of the everyday workings of Sydney multiculturalism, the social ethics of the museum as meeting place. This is what we want you to take away from this Museum of Sydney on this historic site of invasion, plunder and exchange.

Ross Gibson has sewn scholarly research into an imagined world of fables and parables for our own time. His writing will enchant you. A sensitive, incisive historian and poet has given eloquent voice to past oceanic voyagers. Maybe you have passed them in Sydney streets as you have done in your dreams?

Peter Emmett

Senior Curator

Museum of Sydney *on the site of first Government House*

And this also
... has been one of the dark places
of the earth.

Joseph Conrad, *Heart of Darkness*

CONTENTS

THE HISTORY OF OUR BREATHING

Most of all,
we need a history of the desires,
curiosities, systems of perception,
and discourses that organise our witnesses
and their testimonies.

Alain Corbin, *Le Territoire du vide*[1]

This book is a literary version of The Bond Store gallery at the Museum of Sydney, a place where some of the characters lurking in objects and urban precincts are summoned out of the past to haggle and hustle their versions of what has happened in a city where quietly astonishing lives take place every day. It is a book of stories and historical fragments rucked and rubbed together so that pungent little flames of fiction lick out from a tinder of records, rumours and artefacts rummaged from the everyday life of colonial Sydney, 1788 to 1850.

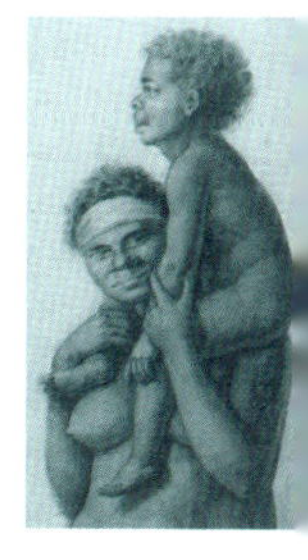

But this book does not present a conventional history, it does not set out to prove anything once and for all. It cannot establish any truths that put an end to argument. Rather it is an attempt to spook out some uncommon memories and some wonderment from the tarnished old lamp of the past so that our present lives might be visible anew in brief flickers of revelation.

Therefore, this is a book for your imagining. It is designed to let you wonder about some of the everyday experiences that have been overlooked in our conventional histories. For example, you might like to imagine how you could tell a history of Australian laughter. Or of Sydney sighs, groans or moans. Limps. Grunts. Agreements. Gestures of hello. Gestures of dismissal, seduction, or shame.

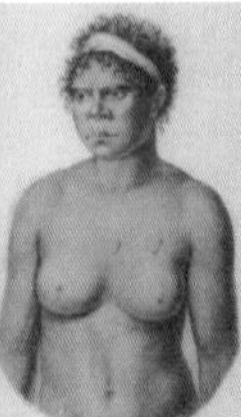

We have to imagine these ordinary mysteries now, because nobody thought to record them methodically in our past. Except for occasional slips of the pen, or nonchalant sketches, private collections or archaeological lucky dips, there is little in the official records that can help us catch the waft of fleeting experiences such as desire and repugnance. The way the past breathed is rarely noted explicitly in the evidentiary systems that historians customarily go to.

But nowadays, in a society full of differences and debts, we are wanting to know ourselves differently and more solvently. People are sensing the need to probe more deeply for the means to know their daily lives.

Once you can see through the accounts of governors, pastoralists and explorers that have defined the colonial past in Australia, you can discern thousands upon thousands of astonishing, unfamiliar events and quandaries. In letters, diaries, footnotes and marginalia, in objects and images, in the shape of the landscape, you can discern traces of the quotidian histories – both indigenous and incursive – that have made Sydney boisterous with contentions and communions. When you look away from the grand history of governance, you can see how the communities that fought and formed in the garrison town were multi-cultural, rambunctious and irresolute. They made their ructions in, around and often despite the pressing ordinance of Government House. What's more, you can begin to see how our multifarious lives today have also been shaped by this ghostly hubbub.

Before, during and after the English seizure of the Port Jackson region, numberless mentalities, appetites and anxieties have haunted Sydney. Such unruly variegation has given the town its character. It has made the place as haunted as it is haunting. Right up to the present day, all these contending urges and repulsions have affected the ways people encounter one another, the ways they cross roads, walk up to shop counters, look and speak to each other, or turn awkwardly away.

The Bond Store is designed to help us muse up a better understanding of these everyday passions and actions. It is a kind of seance-room where we might attach human character and voice to 'dead' chattels that have been traded through Sydney. The gallery is arrayed as a symbolic warehouse where objects that passed though Sydney during the period 1788-1850 are assembled awaiting assessment of their value and payment of their customs fees. It is a haunting-place where we might hear some of the stories embedded in commodities that have touched peoples' past lives. These relics are charms to help us wonder as truly as possible how joy and lust and shame quickened our forbears' pulses and laid down patterns for their breathing, for their wanting and their working. With these objects, these fragments of texts and images, we might begin to know the people of our past better and to know, therefore, how and why we are breathing right now. For the air has been bequeathed to us by the ordinary people of the past. They have already breathed it for us and to us.

So, with such historic air all around us, The Bond Store is designed to be literally inspiring. It is designed as a place of spirit in the original sense of the word – where animating breath can be shown to waft chancily yet vitally through all the elements that form Sydney's human environment. Like the rest of the Museum of Sydney, The Bond Store invites the objects, traces and absences of history to conspire – to breathe together – and thus to murmur in the endlessly debateable proffering of stories about the life of the past in the present so that the past of this place will inspire the present.

A place breathes life so long as it is animated by intrigue and transformation, so long as stories can be told about it. This means we need to muse up stories to help us know the opportunist ocean-town that Sydney was during the first sixty years of colonisation. Such tales are spirited responses to the relics that the past has yielded to us. Regarded collectively, the objects in The Bond Store represent the surreal profusion and conjunction of things and

categories that colonialism brought to the Pacific/Sydney region. Regarded individually, each object 'carries' its stories – about how it got to Sydney, about what human actions and desires have happened around it and persist unexpired in it. The Bond Store stages this interplay between the individual and the political, between subjective conviction and communal ratification. It is a place for wondering how to negotiate the gulfs between what is felt to be true and what is authorised to be true, to wonder what all these little epiphanies might be about.

Notice how we tell stories about places, events and things? A story rarely goes straight to its object. A story tells about its topic and thereby provides shifting vantage-points to prompt a listener's imagination and interpretation. Narrative does not tell straight and true, the way we used to think history did. So, when a group of stories are breathed together about a city, we get a contentious bluster of postulations, a fresh convection of narrative that buffets up truths speculatively, shiftingly and endlessly.

The tales in this book are true stories in as much as they are inspired by material evidence; they are true to the spirit of how people were breathing and enacting all the historically 'nebulous' experiences that vitalise daily life, past and present.

In The Bond Store gallery, visitors cause the phantoms to arise from the objects. As people scrutinise a relic, their proximity triggers a transformation and a ghost arises. Once they have been conjured by curiosity, these phantoms are compelled to tell about the object. The tellers conspire in ever-altering conjunctions, monologue after monologue, so that any one story will always be 'buffeted' by different stories whenever it recurs. The drifts and morals of each tale must alter restlessly, depending on the context that swirls around it. The permutations and combinations of meanings rarely exhaust themselves in the larger pattern of stories that eddy about it. Like the ocean pulsing rhythms for so many cultures that have haggled together in Sydney, the assemblage of strange and chancy combinations in The Bond Store is as productive as it is restless. Or like colonialism itself, the gallery displays a

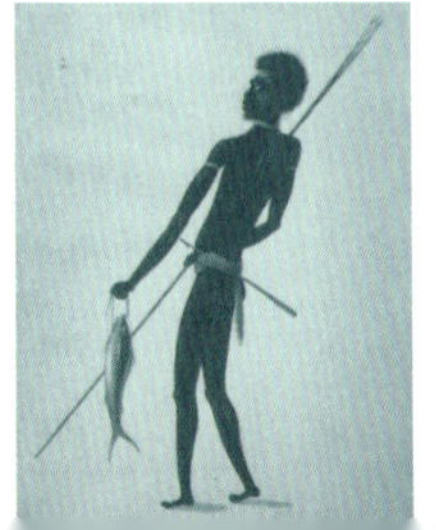

plethora of displaced objects, people and appetites all laying brusque claims on each other in ways that are endlessly unpredictable yet powerfully predicated.

So, as you read this textual version of The Bond Store, you are invited to flick through it back and forth, to draft together your own interrelations of characters and narratives. You are invited to generate theories and meanings out of the contentions and combinations. What happens, for example, when you drift a story across a shoal of other stories, or when historical quotes jibe with fictional propositions, or when genres vie with genres, and biases tack against biases? What can happen when the fleeting elements of everyday life conspire to produce drafts of an imaginable past that are simultaneously true and debateable? As you read this book you are invited to generate ways to chart the truths of daily life looming out of the fictions of possible interpretation.

As one of the characters says at the start of his soliloquy, *most of this story is true.* Just how true and for how long, it's for you to imagine.

1. Alain Corbin, *Le Territoire du vide: l'occident et le desire du rivage (1750 - 1840)*, Paris: Aubier, 1988, p. 22 (my translation).

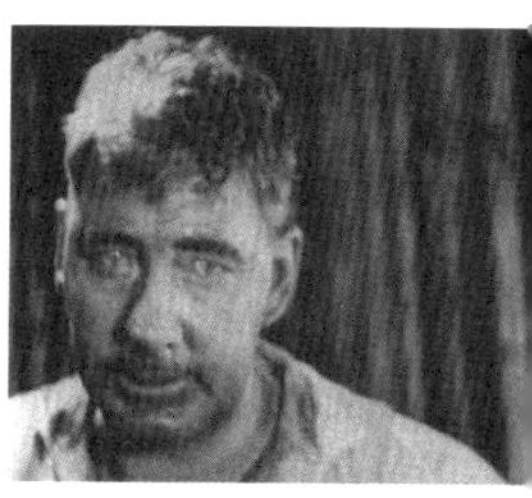

Ross Gibson

SCRIPTS

SENTRY SPIEL

Storyteller: A marine, slightly rum-blind, stands guard at the entrance of the Bond Store

MARINE: *Mind how you step. Watch your head when you walk through the door. We've got everything in store. Everything's waiting in store. Government store. Government bond-store.*[1] *Everything waiting in bond in the store. We store it up here till you pay your bond.*[2] *Pay your customs and break the bond. Pay your customs and break the bond. Why not? These are the customs of our much-esteemed government. This bondage is customary. What good are these things in bond? You want your goods? All goods are in bond. This is our custom. If it's good, it's in bond. If it's good, it's in bond.*

Tortoise-shell combs from Sarawak. Sealskin hats from Canady. Fiji coconuts the size of your head. New Zealand seal oil to rub on your knee. We've got rules for this stuff. Bagged up quantities of subtle pimiento. Oil of vitriol. Lemon-flavoured lozenges. We have reg-u-lated this stuff. If you can't pay the customs, the goods are the Governor's. You want your goods? All goods are in bond.

You don't come into our harbour for nothing. You're in bonds once you get here. You'll meet the tide-waiter, you'll meet the jerquer and the gauger. If they consider you good, they'll put you in bond. They'll add you up and put you in bond. Come to the bond men! Come meet the tide-waiter. Get weighed by the jerquer.

Get measured by the gauger. They'll tally your value. They'll tell you your value.[3]

From the moment you get here, you're engaged in our bonds. In bond to pay the Governor, because he's holding your goods. Me, I'm a bond man. Me, I'm the watcher. I know your value.

Mind how you step. Watch your head. Watch out for the gauger. Watch out for the jerquer. Be good while you're in there. Mind how you step. Watch your head. Watch out for the tide-waiter. Here comes the jerquer. Here comes the gauger. Mind how you step. Watch your head. In you go. In you go. In you go.

Research Notes

The first four Governors of New South Wales – all naval officers – 'had sought to win proper recognition of Sydney as a legitimate naval base and had laboured to keep in commission the few inferior ships at their disposal, on the operation of which much of the colonial business depended. These governors faced a threefold problem comprising the actual duties imposed upon the ships including the import of meat and other provisions from the islands, the creation and maintenance of adequate naval stores and the question of their own status as naval captains while employed as colonial governors.'

John Bach, *The Australia Station: A History of the Royal Navy in the South West Pacific, 1821 - 1913*, Sydney: UNSW Press, 1986, p. 12.

'[Colonial] administrations were concerned to retain or enhance control over land and labour. Superficially, this concern clashed with the judicial and administrative philosophy of contemporary Britain which was imbued with ideas of freedom of contract, freedom of trade and free title to land.'

C. A. Bayly, *Imperial Meridian: The British Empire and the World 1780-1830*, London: Longman, 1989, p. 217.

1. The Bond Store in Sydney was a 'secure warehouse under the supervision of the Customs department for storing goods upon which Customs or excise duties had not been paid.'

David Day, *Smugglers and Sailors: The Customs History of Australia 1788-1901*, Canberra: Australian Government Publishing Services, 1992, p. xxxiii.

There were two Bond Stores in Sergeant Major's Row in the Rocks, opposite the Old Parade Ground near the junction with High Street. Supplies imported by government agencies and by merchants were held in bond until customs duties and landing permits were finalised.

2. The *Macquarie Dictionary* lists twenty-one definitions of 'bond', including:
- something that binds, fastens, confines, or holds together;
- a cord, rope, band, ligament;
- something that unites individual people into a group;
- something that constrains a person to a certain line of behaviour;
- any written obligation under seal;
- the state of dutiable goods on which the duties are unpaid.

3. *Gauger*: 'Customs officer, either in the bond store or on the wharf, who calculated the quantity of spirits, tobacco or other goods upon which Customs duties were to be paid.'

Jerquer: 'Customs officer who checked a ship's papers to ensure that all cargo had been duly entered and properly described. In some cases, jerquers were also responsible for conducting internal audits of the Customs accounts.'

Landing Waiter: 'Customs officer on the wharf charged with checking goods landed against those listed in the ship's manifest.'

Tide Waiter: 'Customs officer who awaited the tide upon which sailing ships might arrive or depart and who then supervised the ships while in port to guard against smuggling or other breaches of the Customs regulations.'

All above glossary definitions are from David Day, *Smugglers and Sailors: The Customs History of Australia 1788-1901*, Canberra: Australian Government Publishing Services, 1992, pp. xxxiv - xxxv.

OUR CANVAS-SACK MAN

Trade Object: Maori patu or ceremonial club
Storyteller: A marine, in his early twenties

MARINE: *At night, if there's a full moon, you can see your shadow in front of you, walking kind of drunk. Your shadow, falling over your feet. You can see things on the ground like you might be under water. And there's noises all around you ... whistling and such. The blacks, whistling and such, so as you know they know about you, how you're under their moon.*

That's the kind of night we found him. A full moon night. A skeleton is what he was. But still in his clothes. Even in his red jacket. Which is strange because of the red and how much the blacks take to the red ... for their old men to be wearing it when they make speeches and such. But here is a man with red clothing and the blacks have not interfered with him. This is to give me the flesh of a goose. A dead man is fright enough. But a dead man so gone to the devil that the blacks will not touch him! Well I ask you! What are we to do?

We pick him up in pieces. We carry him home in a canvas sack.

Mr White, the surgeon, he wants for me to give him the skull, but I will not do that. I am taking the bones away near the water. I will bury him near the water.[1]

And it's there that the blacks come and talk with me. I find I am not frightened! Speaking with them. This is unaccustomed. This very different time. I am not frightened!

The blacks have explanations. They say how they found him in

the first days of our Fleet. He was dying of the runs. Our canvas-sack man.

I have figured him now. His name being Hill. We had always spoken his name like scared men. For the talk in the tents was how he'd been eaten. But here they were, the black men, explaining him to me. He died on his own, as we all do, I suppose. The blacks looking and having no idea what to do with him, what was left of him. The right way to dispose of him, a man who is white and not from their country. How to rest him down? What to do with him? To put him to rest?[2]

They talked with their old people. The ones who wear red. The rules are not clear for them. They decide to let the sun and dirt take him. They leave him on his own. They walk a long way around him.

Ever since I have heard this, I cannot look at these things our merchants bring back from New Zealand.[3] *These heads of brown men that the seal hunters take from the temples to sell to collectors. Have these dead men been put down to rest?*

These statues and teeth. Now, I'm not bowing down to the devil. I'm not like a native.[4] *But why should I be taking any chances with these dead men? What I'm asking is, have they been put to rest? Their ghosts, I mean. These brown men's heads. Their statues, their teeth. Have they been put to rest?*

Research Notes

'Fine weather – after breackfast went up the Harbour in my Boat went a little way up Lane Cove – did not See the two natives that I was with Yesterday – on my way home I Saw a Native on the Shore with two Spears and a throwing Stick in his hand – I cald to him and puld the Boat in towards him but the moment that he Saw that I was coming on Shore he Set off as if the Devil was after him – I land[ed] and took my Gun and made Ellis and my two Convict men doe the Same after making the Boat fast and we went a little way in the wood but could not See or heer any thing of the Native – on Returning back to the Boat I found the Skeleton of a man or Woman – the Skin was Still entire on the back part of the Head and the Hair Still adhering to it which was in colour of light Brown from which I was certain that it could be non of the natives but must belong to Some Unfortunate person that was Kild by the Natives or what is much more dreadful than being Kild by the Natives that of lossing oneself and perishing with hunger – it Struck me as it did every body in the Boat that [it] must be the skeleton of Mr. Hill a midshipman belonging to the Sirius who was either Kild by the Natives or lost in the woods – I brought the head home with me and sent it to the Hospital to see if the[y] could inform me if it was a Natives or one of the people that has been missing when it proves to be the Head of one Hill a convict that was loss from Rose Hill near a twelf month Since – The Surgeons wanted for me to give them the Skull but I would not – I told them that I would carry it back and collect the rest of the Bons and Bury them and the Head –'

Ralph Clark, *The Journal and Letters of Lt. Ralph Clark 1787-1792* (edited by Paul G. Fidlon and R. J. Ryan), Sydney: Australian Documents Library, 1981, entry for Tuesday, 16th Feb., 1790, p. 110.

'The demand for bodies, itself a product of the renovation in medicine and medical teaching that began in the Paris hospitals of the 1790s, came from doctors. The new anatomical-pathological model of disease required an intimate knowledge of the body's structures, particularly organs. In the 1790s when demand was still relatively low "the price of a subject", as it was called, was between 1 gn. and 3 gn.'

Thomas Laqueur, 'Bodies, Death and pauper Funerals', in *Representations*, 1 (Feb., 1983), p. 123.

1. '[Between] about 1750 and 1850, the commemoration of the soul's departure from the body and the body's return to dust became an occasion to represent, with unrivalled clarity, the possibility of social worthlessness, earthly failure, and profound anonymity. For the same reasons that the well appointed funerals of the wealthy and prominent came to signify their pre-eminent position in society, the ignominious funerals of the poor came to signify the opposite – their absolute exclusion from the social body.'

Thomas Laqueur, 'Bodies, Death and pauper Funerals', in *Representations*, 1 (Feb., 1983), p. 109.

2. 'In a world ... where public standing had become ultimately linked to the importance one had earned in the eyes of one's fellow men, no man's reputation could be finally assured until the moment of his death. Funerals thus became the ritual occasions for definitively marking social place, and the imaginative vehicle for contemplating one's ultimate fate in the public eye. For the rich and successful, for those with social ties, the funeral could be contemplated with equanimity. Not so for the poor and friendless; it haunted them as the spectre of failure.'

Thomas Laqueur, 'Bodies, Death and pauper Funerals', in *Representations*, 1 (Feb., 1983), p. 109.

3. 'EVENING SALE. At Messrs. Paul's Auction Rooms, THIS EVENING, the Sale to commence at Seven o'Clock, when, will be sold, a great variety of Goods, consisting of RICH CUT and PLAIN GLASS, plated goods, cutlery, and japan ware. Wearing apparel, superfine hats, &c. Also, THE CURIOSITIES lately imported by the Bee, comprising SPEARS, CLUBS, New Zealand and other MATS, SHELLS, &c.'

Sydney Gazette, July 2, 1831.

4. 'During the three and a half centuries after 1500 ... the religion of European seafarers and seafaring communities challenged and was challenged by the forces of modernity and responded in a variety of ways, often passively and indifferently, but sometimes with fierce resistance. Far from being characterised by traditional piety, orthodoxy and conservative spirituality, the active Christianity found by folklorists and ethnographers among many maritime communities in the late eighteenth century was of relatively recent origin ... If European sailors were religious, their religion comprised a curious amalgam of magic, necromancy, witchcraft and Christian and para-Christian beliefs and practices.'

James Pritchard, 'Roundtable: Alain Cabantous', in *International Journal of Maritime History, Vol. III*, No. 1 (1991), pp. 180 - 81.

A MAN ALWAYS IN CHECK

Trade Object: Chess pieces carved from sandalwood
Storyteller: A French woman, late forties

WOMAN: *I loved some men on Mauritius. French men of wealth and plantation. Or I thought I did at that time, when I was young and I saw in them the way I wished to see myself. And I had pleasures in my person which they patronised well, in the early days at least. For it was a place, Mauritius, where pleasure was a rule amongst the free and the wealthy. You see, there were slaves everywhere then, for pain and for arduous things.*

But pleasure is not only hand on flesh and so on. And I was soon out of delight with these plantation men. You know, the delights of conversation, and so on.

In those days on the island there was an English man, the name of Flinders, retained on our island because of our war with the English.[1] *His boat leaking offshore. He called out for assistance. For years he was sealed up here in detention, because his ship was not sealed well. He had with him a cat and a set of pieces for chess contests.*

This was an island devoted to pleasure, remember. And I was not happy in my liaisons. Therefore to sit and play chess with such a man, young and incarcerated, would be a way to have gossip, a way to steal pleasure, from a man young and ardent, in so much confinement.

But Mr Flinders was not conventional. A man with thirty years, he appeared to have seventy in his face and his frame. Pleasure was a sad thing to contemplate with him. Bodily pleasure. One could not take it from him, so little did he have in his person.

No gossip could speak ill of him, for it was so plain how he was. His lust was with maps, and for his name upon maps.[2] *He had love, he told me, for a wife back in London. Ten years since they had touched. As if once they gave pleasure and took breath from each other. And here he was now, in front of me, this man wearing so many years. And his maps taken from him. And talking to his cat.*[3] *And looking at me, who is accustomed to the carnal thinking of men, and who is seeing no danger coming from Mr Flinders.*

Why does a man take such risks with his pleasures? I mean to take coastlines and surveys for his lovers? When he has flesh and blood he may touch? Mine, which he might touch! I asked him this question. I asked him two times. But he seemed not to hear me.

His chess was defensive. He made no adventure on the board. Every man was moved warily. He took no delight in protecting his king and his queen.

I once had a sailor. During this time. I made his acquaintance. A favour I asked him ... to carve a chess set for me, from sandalwood root. For Mr Flinders, to bring him some pleasure.

I played one game with my sailor, before offering the chessmen to Mr Flinders. My sailor was reckless. Easily conquered. Perhaps he was making efforts to please me. Each time I claimed a man and took it in my hand a warm fragrance wafted on the board. It was so very ... unctuous. These sandalwood armies.

I could not give this thing to Mr Flinders. You know the way a fragrance might break into your heart? A brief intimation of perfume, and your day is destroyed.

I am told he has died now. Not long after returning. Mr Flinders. To England, I mean, where his wife was there waiting. I am told he has died now.

Research Notes

1. Having set out on his return voyage to England in September 1803, Matthew Flinders was unaware that hostilities between England and France were about to exacerbate. By the time his afflicted ship sought refuge and repair in Mauritius, war had flared between the nations. Flinders was astonished to be seized as a spy and a dangerous enemy.

2. Knowing that Flinders was devoted to his vocation as a surveyor of coastlines, the French authorities on Mauritius took possession of all his maps and charts. He was thus constrained more emphatically than any imprisonment could ever effect.

3. Flinders' cat, Trim, about whom he wrote a memorial book, was born in 1799 on board the ship *Roundabout*, on a voyage between the Cape of Good Hope and Port Jackson. The cat accompanied Flinders on most of his ventures, including the voyage back to England which was so unexpectedly curtailed at Mauritius. Trim went missing while being cosseted by a French girl on Mauritius. The disappearance affected Flinders deeply.

Flinders was released on June 13, 1810, after seven and a half years of confinement on the island.

After the British took charge of Mauritius, in July 1810, Flinders was free to make his way back to England. Although he was in his late thirties when he arrived in London, old acquaintances were shocked to see a man worn out and frail, resembling a septuagenarian. He lived long enough to see his journal and life story get set up for the printing press. He died within days of its publication.

For thorough accounts of Flinders' fate, see Edward Duyker, *Of the Star and the Sea: Mauritius: Mauritians and Australia*, Sydney: Australian Mauritian Research Group, 1988, and Geoffrey Ingleton, *Matthew Flinders: Navigator and Chartmaker*, Guildford: Genesis, 1986.

IN THE EYES OF AN ALBATROSS

Trade Object: A water colour painting
Storyteller: An English painter sketching in a workbook

PAINTER: *Walk out under the sun, you're sure to meet a character. Sydney Town is bulging with them. Which is my good fortune. I am a painter.*[1] *It is my good fortune to visit your town. People in England will buy you from me.*

Yes, wherever you go you're sure to meet a character.[2] *Not so long ago I was less comfortable than I am now. For eight months I was marooned on an island in the Atlantic. TRISTAN DA CUNHA! Who is on this place? A few dissolute castaways. Why does this place exist? That's the first question I asked myself there.*

There was a day I went hunting, out in the hills. For nourishment, yes. But for diversion, principally. To kill something so I could feel less like I was dying. I went with the castaways, who were not alive in a way I could approve. So, yes, your question has merit: 'Why did I think that killing with them would invigorate me?' Ahh! ... How can you think well in places like that?

I became separated from my companions. I could hear them caterwauling off down the valley. 'I wandered lonely as a cloud.' Until I came upon a pair of albatross. Do you know the size of these birds? How formidable they are? I mean they have characteristics and bulk to compare with yourself. Why was I up there on that hill? For hunting, remember. In my mind I was obliged to bring back a trophy. You ask me, 'Who would eat an

albatross?' And I ask you, 'Have you spent time in places like that?' Well!

So here were my trophies. I pounded the first one in its head. It honked and fell over. I turned to take the other one ... and it stood there and looked at me. It looked at me and then lent its head forward. As if it was offering itself.

But by now my blood had come down. My mind also had come back. What had I done? A dead bird lay there with no head on its neck. Had I done this? Well, yes. These things are done in the world. Such force is how things proceed in the world. Good, the pulse of my thinking had brought my blood back.

I took up my club, and the remaining bird now raised up its head from where it had been gazing on its dead partner.[3] *Now it looked me in my eye. It looked straight into me. I think I dropped the club. In the eyes of a bird I had met my own character. I turned away. But it walked urgently at me. It was following me! With its head pushed out forward.*

If I could reverse time, I would take back those five minutes and raise up both birds. Leave them there, swaggering. But this is what I've learned about things done in the world. What's done is done. You can try to paint over it. But the things you've done, the things you've done, the things you've done, they'll follow you home and look you in the eye.

Research Notes

1. Augustus Earle is the historical figure who prompted this tale. He was a travelling artist who spent several months in Sydney during his independent voyage around the world in the late 1820s.

See Jocelyn Hackforth Jones, *Augustus Earle, Travel Artist; paintings and drawings in the Rex Nan Kivell Collection,* Canberra: National Library of Australia, 1980. See also Augustus Earle, *Narrative of a Residence in New Zealand; Journal of a Residence in Tristan da Cunha,* Oxford: Clarendon Press, 1966.

Earle himself became a Sydney celebrity. Newspapers reported his activities extensively. For example, on October 4, 1827, the *Monitor* announced that 'Mr Earle is at present engaged in painting a comprehensive view of Sydney, from the North Shore, for a nobleman in England.' And two years later the *Gazette* was still recalling how Earle's Sydney sojourn had leavened cultural life in the colony: '[Mr Earle's George Street gallery was] ... much visited by the youth of the Colony, and must have a considerable influence in promoting good taste among the rising generation.'

2. Whilst in Sydney, Earle met several 'colourful Sydney identities'. As a result of this conviviality, he painted a portrait of Bungaree, the Aboriginal mediator who became a celebrity in Sydney and England. As the Russian mariner and scientist, F. G. Bellingshausen, observed in 1820, Bungaree insisted on being in the 'welcoming party' for all new ships arriving in Port Jackson. In a small boat crewed by Aboriginal colleagues, Bungaree would often beat the Harbourmaster on to the ships and would address the new arrivals with a sweep of his arms and a confident declamation: 'These are my people ... This is my land.'

See Keith Vincent Smith, *King Bungaree. A Sydney Aborigine meets the great South Pacific Explorers, 1799-1830,* Sydney: Kangaroo Press, 1992.

Many whites tried to slander Bungaree as a buffoon. But Earle seems to have realised the importance and canniness of Bungaree.

The portrait shows a witty man whose face and gestures are poised with irony and charm. Perhaps Earle was always ready to interpret people and events against the grain of popular preconception. This is probably how he earned his reputation as 'our unpuritanical artist'.

See *Quarterly Review*, October 1832.

3. Albatrosses are almost invariably 'monogamous'. A female and male mate for life, and if one dies the other rarely takes a new partner.

See Mildred L. Fisher, *Albatross of Midway Island: a natural history of the Laysan Albatross*, Carbondale: Southern Illinois University Press, 1970.

See also R. J. Tomkins, *Attendance of wandering albatrosses (Diomedea exulans) at a small colony on Macquarie Island*, Kingston (Tas.): Department of Science, Antarctic Division, 1985.

'I remember the first albatross I ever saw. It was during a prolonged gale, in waters hard upon the Antarctic seas. From my forenoon watch below, I ascended to the overclouded deck; and there, dashed upon the main hatches, I saw a regal, feathery thing of unspotted whiteness, and with a hooked, Roman bill sublime ... Though bodily unharmed, it uttered cries, as some king's ghost in supernatural distress. Through its inexpressible, strange eyes, methought I peeped to secrets which took hold of God. As Abraham before the angels, I bowed myself ...'

Herman Melville, *Moby-Dick*, first published 1851, Chapter XLII, 'The Whiteness of the Whale'.

THESE ARE ALL NEW SPECTACLES FOR THE PEOPLE IN EUROPE

Trade Object: A steel machete
Storyteller: A young Sydney entrepreneur

MERCHANT: *What do people want? STRANGE is what people want. When they go out for entertainment, I mean. There's money abounding in the pockets of a fairground crowd. What do they want? Answer this question correctly, and put your hand out for their money.*

What new things have come into the world? The brown people of the south seas. That's one thing. But there's shows with them already. Capering and caterwauling.

What else is new? European industry and the machines that make our great wealth.[1] *These blades made of metal. These tools of such bite. Well they have seen such things, the crowds in the fairgrounds. But have they seen what these machines can do? To a brown man or woman? Now, who has seen this? As we triumph in the south seas, with our engines and implements, what do we produce. In our whale ships. In our man-o-wars.*[2] *In our plantations and produce-fields. What have we produced that I can put on show?*

These things are passing strange. The half-men, the amputees and cripples that we have constructed by industry.[3] *The brown men and women persisting in pieces. Hobbling and leaning. Living and breathing with so little of them remaining. These are a wonderment to your fairground crowd.*

Here is a show to end all the shows!!

Research Notes

1. Just as the First World War brought new technologies of destruction to European communities and therefore forced Europeans to acknowledge new definitions of the body as a thing which could be dismembered and reconstituted, so the arrival – a century earlier – of European industry in the South Pacific brought radically new bodily and social integrations and disintegrations to indigenous societies all over the Pacific. A honed steel blade, for one thing, introduced indigenous communities to unaccustomed new experiences of work and pain.

See James M. Mellard, *The Exploded Form; the modernist novel in America*, Urbana: University of Illinois Press, 1980.

As industrial accidents became more common, methods of palliative amputation and suture began to be refined also. Survivors of such operations became objects of scientific and popular fascination ... ... 'The bodies of the poor, in the most literal, physical sense of body, became the badge of their condition. The evils of the new industrial system, of mine and factory, were clearly manifest in the bent spines, legs and arms of children who were measured and recorded by scores of social investigators.'

Thomas Laqueur, 'Bodies, Death and Pauper Funerals', in *Representations*, 1(Feb. 1983), p. 123.

Wherever European industrialisation met indigenous societies in the early stages of colonisation, the metal machines bit into brown bodies. ... ... 'At Habana [in the sugar-milling country of Central Queensland] in 1883, an ignorant kanaka feeding the rollers, decided to rest his foot on the pinion driving the mill. His leg was swiftly drawn into the machinery and as he clung to the pinion his left arm and leg were torn off.'

John Kerr, *Pioneer Pageant: A History of the Pioneer Shire*, Mackay: Pioneer Shire Council, 1980, p. 86.

See also Robert Bogdan, *Freak Show: presenting human oddities for amusement and profit*, Chicago: University of Chicago Press, 1988.

See also Martin Howard, *Victorian Grotesque: an Illustrated Excursion into Medical Curiosities, Freaks and Abnormalities – Principally of the Victorian Age*, London: Jupiter, 1977.

2. '[During a warship battle, one] of our poor fellows was cut in two by a double-headed shot on the main deck and [the] lining of his stomach (about the size of a pancake) stuck on the side of the launch, which was stowed amidships on the main deck with the sheep inside. The butcher who had the care of them, observing what was on the side of the boat, began to scrape it off with his nails, saying, "Who the devil would have thought the fellow's paunch would have stuck so? I'm damned if I don't think it's glued on!"'

James Anthony Gardner, *Above and Under Hatches: being Naval Recollections in shreds and patches with strange reflections, written in 1836*, edited by Christopher Lloyd, London: Batchworth, 1955, p. 21.

3. 'By machines mankind are able to do that which their own bodily powers would never effect to the same extent. Machines are the produce of the mind of man; and, their existence distinguishes the civilized man from the savage. The savage has no machines, or, at least, nothing that we call machines.'

William Cobbett, 'A Letter to the Luddites' in his *Political Register*, XXXI, (1816), p. 561.

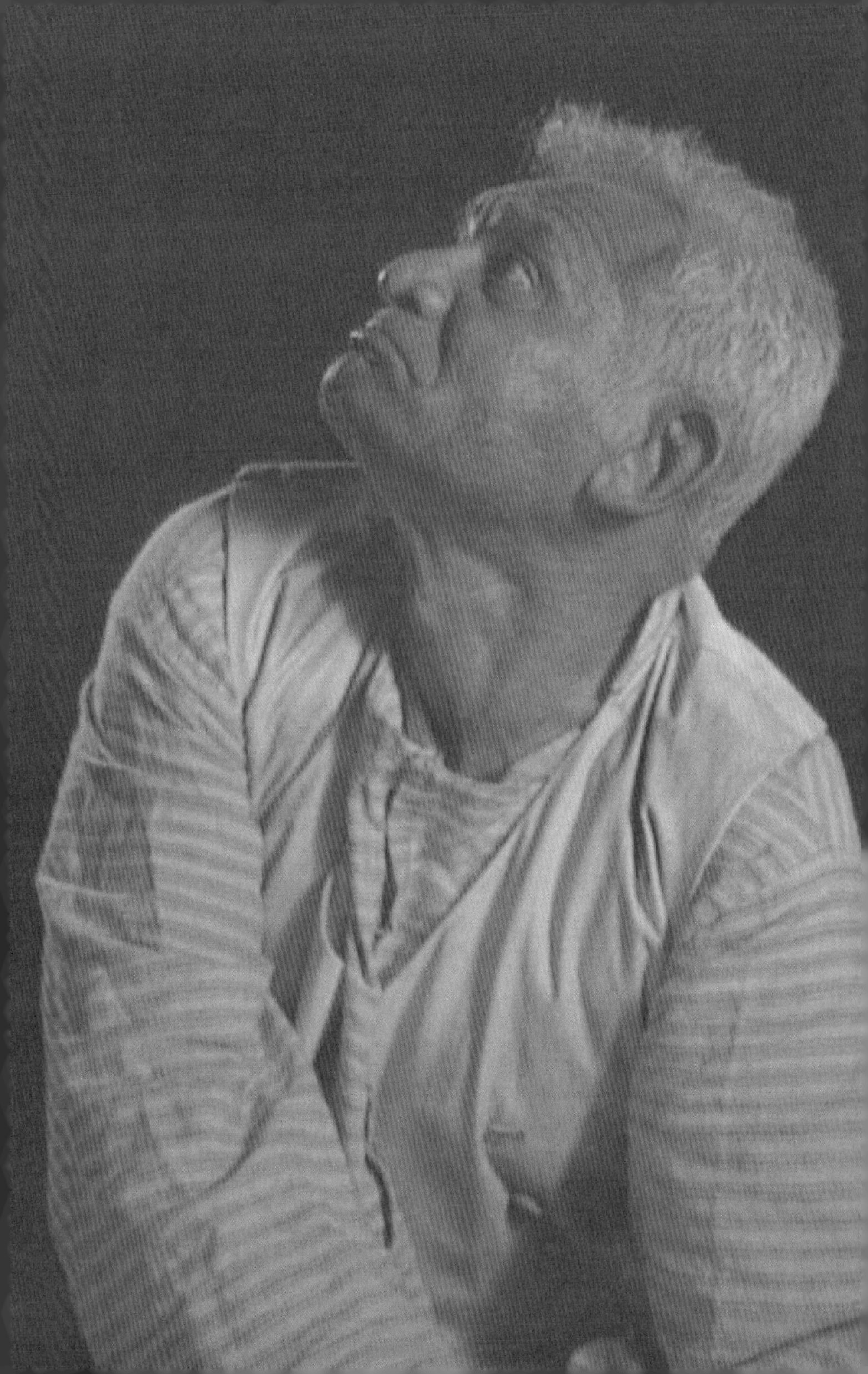

BON-DEL TELLS ME

Trade Object: Salon lamp fuelled by whale oil
Storyteller: A Ceylonese merchant sailor

SAILOR: *Most of this story is true. In 1804 I was on the* Astrophel, *chasing the whale in Tahitian waters. We were fish-following men from every part of the world. Most of us walking on to the ship in Sydney Town, from boarding houses in the Rocks, where we had occasion to roister between months under sail. We had amongst our crew all the pinks and blotches that are called 'white' of the skin, and all the shades of tan and pigment that some men must wear as 'black' for their skin as well as for their luck. Called 'black' and graded in misfortune like this by the white men. Black skin, black luck. And we had yellow men too. We were all kinds.*

We had a Port Jackson boy, called black by some, called Bon-del by himself.[1] *A native of the harbour. His mother was bit apart by a shark with a head shaped like a hammer. This is true. It was ten years ago, when Bon-del was all legs and arms. Seven years old. We knew him even in those days, because he got celebrated: the Governor sent him to Norfolk Island, because he was an orphan then ... the shark with his mother, the pox with the father. So he's seven and he's on a boat for Norfolk, learning ropes and sails and ways to climb down. 'To get a trade,' the Governor said.*[2] *But to tell secrets about his language and his people too, Bon-del says nowadays, talking like a wise young man.*

But he learned the sea, did Bon-del, and here he was ten years

older and looking to get rich out of twenty-five whales. Which number would be bounty if we fastened on to so many. And this much is possible during months under sail, in the South Sea, on the roads where the big fish takes his way through the world.

The islander men – Hawaiians and Maoris with great arms on harpoons – they used this word: 'Roads'.[3] *They said, 'The ocean has roads.' They would say this to the captain. The Captain would smile and nod, like at a child. The men with the arms would say they would not get rich this time, not if the Captain smiled childish at the roads.*

They said all this like a dog might talk. Bits of words from English tongue, bits from their own, barked and short. The Captain maintained, 'THAT HE WOULD NOT TALK LIKE A DOG'. But it's something I learned to do. And I find a dog must know more than some creatures on hind legs.[4]

Bon-del knew English words. And he knew Dog, which he offered to me, as a token of friendship.

All men are different. I'm here to tell you. Different by dint of their various homelands and the ways they were used in the worlds of their boyhoods. But every man is a man too if you speak with him of appetite. In talking of lust or defilement you'll find your mind taking part with all strange manner of men. So Bon-del and I commenced with talking of wanting. Which made between us a sensible Equality. All this in the English he picked up on Norfolk. The same language I picked up on ships owned by Englanders. And when we were friends, he took me to talk Dog with the men from the islands.

They would speak about hunting, Bon-del explaining that a man does not look for a kangaroo, nor does he chase it. A man must go out into country and take instruction from the ground

and sniff at the wind and move in the only way the day will let him go. Like the day was instruction. Then a good hunter will look up sometime in the day and the kangaroo will be there, each waiting for the other.

The men with the harpoons, they would nod with assent: it's the same with the fish.

When I made report to the captain – changing Dog words into English – he laughed like a father. He said it was his task to look. And he thanked God for being a white man.

I'll tell you this much. All through those months, all over the roads of that watery world, we caught no kind of fish, no matter what pains we took in looking and chasing.

Research Notes

Many Australian Aborigines went deep sea sailing and some were reported to have spent time on pelagic whaling ships.

See N. Gunson (ed.), *Australian reminiscences and papers of L. E. Threlkeld: missionary to the Aborigines*, 2 vols (Canberra: ANU Pacific Linguistic Series B, 1990), Vol. I, pp. 78 - 9.

'[The] exploits of our whalers were a part of "the great reaching out" which filled in the outline of our coast and put dots on our remote interior. Land explorers set out in search of new pastures and settlement followed. Whalers reached out in search of new whaling grounds and settlement followed.'

Max Colwell, *Whaling Around Australia*, Adelaide: Rigby, 1969, pp. 103 - 4.

Whaling vessels became known colloquially as 'black ships' because the decks and sails were always begrimed with soot from the boiling-down vats which were continually being fired on the decks. One could smell the black ships miles off, even before they hove into view, and in many ports, because of their stench, they were assigned to sectors of the harbour well away from residential areas.

See E.W. Clement, 'Mito Samurai and British Sailors in 1824', in *Transactions of the Asiatic Society of Japan*, Vol. 33, Part I, July 1905, p. 87.

August 3, 1832 – '5 whalers, all fully equipped and well-manned go to sea tomorrow upon a whaling cruise. Wish them every success. "These and the wool bales – are our national sinews ...".'

The Australian, August 3, 1832.

1. March 22, 1791 – '[The] indefatigable Supply again sailed for Norfolk Island, carrying thither captain Hill, and a detachment of the New South Wales corps. A little native boy, named Bon-del, who had long particularly attached himself to captain Hill, accompanied him, at his own request. His father had been killed in battle, and his mother bitten in two by a shark: so that he was an orphan, dependant on the humanity of his tribe for protection.'

Watkin Tench, *Sydney's First Four Years*, Sydney: Library of Australian History, 1979.

2. Boys were commonly taken on long voyages. Nimbleness, physical resilience and general emotional effervescence – qualities customarily ascribed to youth – were presumed to be beneficial on a long cruise. Also, a voyage could be regarded both by the children and by the navy as an informal kind of apprenticeship in the numberless ways of the ocean and profitable seafaring. Thus, by the late eighteenth century, a 'line-of-battle ship might have on board fifty or more boys aged from six to eighteen.'

N. A. M. Rodger, *The Wooden World: An Anatomy of the Georgian Navy*, Annapolis, Maryland: Naval Institute Press, 1986, p. 68.

3. '[Islanders] saw the Pacific as a sea of islands or a highway ... whereas continental humans see it more as an expanse of empty ocean.'

Geoffrey Irwin, *The Prehistoric Exploration and Colonisation of the Pacific*, Cambridge: Cambridge University Press, 1992, p. 54.

Ocean 'road' navigation is a sophisticated science among many islander societies. The sea provides a profusion of signs which can be interpreted by a navigator who has 'imbibed' years of experiential training in the presence of mariners who embody the knowledge. The signs can be read in almost every element of the ocean environment: the relational motion of the moon and the stars over several nights duration; systematic comparisons of the risings and settings of the sun and the moon; water colour; drift objects; bird behaviour; phosphorescence in water; the luminance of distant landmasses reflected in clouds; the shape and directional changes of wave-lines in relation to wind direction as waves refract around far-off landmasses; the different smells of open sea, fishing grounds, reefs and islands.

See Geoffrey Irwin, *The Prehistoric Exploration and Colonisation of the Pacific*, Cambridge: Cambridge University Press, 1992 and Will Kyselka, *An Ocean in Mind*, Honolulu: University of Hawaii Press, 1987. See also R. Downs and D. Stea, *Maps in Minds: Reflections on Cognitive Mapping*, New York: Harper & Row, 1977.

4. 'Whaling in the Pacific was the first enterprise which brought English-speaking people into extended contact with Pacific Island people, and promoted the development of contact languages in that area. The high seas whaling industry began in the Pacific after the

1788 voyage of the British whaler Emilia around Cape Horn, returning to England in 1790 with a full cargo of sperm oil from the south Pacific ... American and other British ships soon followed.'

Jakelin Troy, *Australian Aboriginal Contact with the English Language in New South Wales 1788 to 1845*, Canberra: A.N.U. Research School of Pacific Studies and the Department of Linguistics, 1990, p. 20.

The 'immersed', holistic way of knowing one's way through the ocean seems to have philosophical and practical similarities with the knowledge that informs the hunting procedures of many tribal societies. After years of living and working in the Arctic circle, for example, Barry Lopez offers this understanding of Eskimo hunting techniques:

'Hunting in my experience – and by hunting I simply mean being out on the land – is a state of mind. All of one's faculties are brought to bear in an effort to become fully incorporated into the landscape. It is more than listening for animals or watching for hoofprints or a shift in the weather. It is more than an analysis of what one senses. To hunt means to have the land around you like clothing. To engage in a wordless dialogue with it, one so absorbing that you cease to talk with your human companions. It means to release yourself from rational images of what something "means" and to be concerned only that it "is". And then to recognise that things exist only insofar as they can be related to other things. These relationships – fresh drops of moisture on top of rocks at a river crossing and a raven's distant voice – become patterns. The patterns are always in motion. Suddenly the pattern – which includes physical hunger, a memory of your family, and memories of the valley you are walking through, these particular plants and smells – takes in the caribou. There is a caribou standing in front of you. The release of the arrow or bullet is like a word spoken out loud. It occurs at the periphery of your concentration. ... The focus of a hunter in a hunting society was not killing animals but attending to the myriad relationships he understood bound him into the world he occupied with them.'

Barry Lopez, *Arctic Dreams: Imagination and Desire in a Northern Landscape*, New York: Charles Scribner's Sons, 1986, pp. 199 - 200.

See also, L. G. Churchward, 'Notes on American Whaling Activities in Australian Waters 1800-1850', in *Historical Studies*, Nov. 1949.

CAN YOU BE THIS UNLUCKY?

Trade Object: Iron fencing post
Storyteller: A ship's carpenter

CARPENTER: *Have you seen a thunderbolt on the ocean?*[1] *Have you seen what it can do?*

A few years ago I was the carpenter for a two-master on a run to Peru. We're coming back home. And a storm knocks us over.[2] *It just falls out of the blue sky. Lightning like cannon fire. The mainmast comes down at the middle. Out there in the ocean, a tree drops on our heads!*

Sure, this is all bad luck. But there's good luck as well. Because we're close to Norfolk Island[3] *Where they've got their pine trees. Straight and tall like a mast.*

We get one aboard. A pine tree. Now this is no carnival. Because there's no harbour to speak of. It's a day spent in rowboats. Two days of block and tackle. It's the biggest piece of timber.

But we get it all working. And we're four days out of Sydney. When another storm comes and gets us. Like it was the first one been hiding up there in the heavens, watching us, waiting. But this time the mast doesn't fall down like 'TIMBER'. This time it flies into ten thousand pieces, like one long keg of gunpowder.

Norfolk Island! What use is this place! The pine trees splinter when you look at them. And the flax that they grow there, it snaps off in short handfuls. There's no fabric you can make from it.

Norfolk Island![4] *Don't say that name to a man in the navy! Whose idea was Norfolk Island?*

But what is our plan now? We're in the middle of the ocean. We've got one little mast left. And I'm sure that old storm, it's still up there.

So I go tell the captain how I'm getting nervous. He says, well go on and get nervous, what else can you do?

So I act on my inklings. We've got fence posts, iron fence posts in the cargo. Mexican bargains. And I've got Faraday[5] *and Ben Franklin in my memory. From my long nights of reading.*

Here's what to do. I climb up the little mast. I'm holding wire and a fence post. I lash the post to the topmast and run the wire down to the water.[6] *Now everybody looks at me like the sun's cooked my reason.*

But two days later, the storm comes back down and gets us. It throws down its thunderbolts. Only, this time we come through and the mast it's still standing.

In his books, Ben Franklin, he calls it the 'lightning conductor'. It's this way he explains it: the air gets irate and it strikes at the metal, but the wire takes all the anger and sends it away. For us the ocean took all the air's anger.

Well, ring the all the town's bells! We make it to Sydney with a fence-post at our tops! See the news, how it runs around, how we've been in bad luck and good luck. And nobody laughs nasty now, nobody laughs nasty when I sit down with my books.

Research Notes

1. During the late eighteenth century, many different theories were circulating about both the nature of lightning and the best protective procedures. All over Europe, scores of sextons and priests were killed during bell ringing rituals which were meant to ward off lightning during electrical storms. (According to present-day theories of lightning, working so closely to elevated, unearthed metal would be the worst thing to do in a storm.) It was presumed that there was a causal connection between lightning strikes and earthquakes. Natural philosophers debated the best way to recognise and predict 'earthquake weather'.

During the 1750s, in Europe, the first ground-conducted lightning rods were installed as experiments with electrical current. Similar experiments made Benjamin Franklin famous in the American colonies. Indeed, in 1773 when visiting London, Franklin was surprised to find that lightning rods were being attached to many buildings.

See I. Bernard Cohen, *Benjamin Franklin's Science*, Cambridge (Mass): Harvard University Press, 1990.

2. 'The upper air burst into life!
And a hundred fire-flags sheen,
To and fro they hurried about!
And to and fro, and in and out,
The wan stars danced between.

And the coming wind did roar more loud,
And the sails did sigh like sedge;
And the rain poured down from one black cloud;
The moon was at its edge.

The thick black cloud was cleft, and still
The Moon was at its side:
Like waters shot from some high crag,

The lightning fell with never a jag,
A river steep and wide.

Samuel Taylor Coleridge, 'The Rime of the Ancient Mariner', 1798, Part V, ll. pp. 313 - 326.

3. 'Norfolk Island was seized on early as a possible supplier of timber, until it was found that the magnificent pine growing on the island was too brittle for masts and the harbour too hazardous for shipping.'

Margaret Steven, *Trade, Tactics and Territory: Britain in the Pacific 1783-1823*, Melbourne: Melbourne University Press, 1983, p. 125.

4. Norfolk Island was as much a curse as an extension to the New South Wales colony during the early decades. Philip Gidley King's journal of the garrison's early days there betray his nervous concerns about the spirit of the place. It was a location where, for days on end, one had to watch the 'Surf continuing suspicious', a place where geographical and geological characteristics (the preponderance of pumice stone, for example) suggested that the island existed because of 'some great shock of nature' and presumably could withdraw into the ocean just as brusquely as it had emerged.

See Paul G. Fidlon and R. J. Ryan (eds), *The Journal of Philip Gidley King, R. N. 1787 - 1790*, Sydney: Australian Documents Library, 1980, p. 149 and p. 46.

5. The publication of the first volume of Michael Faraday's Experimental Researches in Electricity occurred in 1839.

6. In London in 1843, William Snow Harris published *On the Nature of Thunderstorms.* For at least a decade previously, Harris had petitioned the Royal Navy to fit lightning rods to the masts of all ships. By 1840, several ships were experimentally equipped.

See also C. Maxwell Cade and Delphine Davis, *The Taming of Thunderbolts: The Science and Superstition of Ball Lightning*, London: Abelard-Schuman, 1969.

See also Thomas Burnet, *The Theory of the Earth*, London, 1684.

CONSIDER YOURSELF

Trade Object: A hand mirror
Storyteller: An old merchandising man

MAN: *In the early days, we had to sell anything. Because people here had nothing. Whatever came in on the ships, no matter what it was, you could be sure somebody didn't have it, or there was so much they didn't have that they'd buy any nonsense, just to know for themselves that they had something.*

But mirrors! Now this is a strange thing. Even in those days – 'the acquisitive days' I call them – even then you could never be sure you'd sell a mirror. You had to be ready to try all kinds of trickery. Some customers were easy: men who were proud of their deeds, they were always ready to appraise themselves. But there were people who had this look in their eye. A kind of flicker. In their eyes you could see they had a candle caught in the wind. Like there was something they could almost remember. Like their light could go out at any time. These people, they'd weaken now and then and ask themselves what they were doing here. You couldn't get them to look at themselves in a mirror. Their eyes looking down.

Most likely you could sell them sherry or rum. And we always had plenty of that.

Research Notes

'What all [the early Governors] wished to discountenance were the extremes of profit-taking which the absence of currency and the location of the colonies on developing Pacific trade routes had made possible. Ruthless, laissez-faire business practices, devoted to the short-term profits of local speculators, might serve to secure for British manufacturers sources of raw materials, but they also jeopardized the experiment in convict colonization and the interests of the British ruling class.'

Jan Kociumbas, *The Oxford History of Australia. Volume Two: 1770-1860. Possessions*, Melbourne: Oxford University Press, 1992, p. 106.

'After the loss of its American empire multiple forces played upon the British government and threatened the coherence of its policies. It was a different world for the merchant as well as the politician. In the period of recession and intense foreign competition that characterised the years after 1783 both were compelled to look beyond traditional markets.'

Margaret Steven, *Trade, Tactics and Territory: Britain in the Pacific 1783-1823*, Melbourne: Melbourne University Press, 1983, p. ix.

DO NOT CHATTER IN USELESS ARGOT

Trade Object: Maritime signal flags
Storyteller: Market spruiker

SPRUIKER: *My friends, civilised endeavour requires a sophistication of mind not customary amongst the native peoples of this region. A good sailor is a man of science and scientific tasks require a mind nourished and informed by language dedicated to commercial endeavour. A sailor on board one of our floating worlds must have his good language. Otherwise, you might as well be warbling polynesian! Or chattering in the argot of a Devonshire ploughman!*

We must bring right language into the ocean of your mind! I have here with me the best Dictionary of Sea Terms, *newly arrived from England. Its language must be mastered by any young man who follows the mast into our South Seas. Do you know these words?*

Arm, apron, bilge, single spanish burton, dog-vane, drabler, glut, gudgeon, gooseneck, grommet.

Do you know these words? Who amongst you wants to be a sailor? Without good language you are worse than useless in the islands. You can make no account unless you have verbiage with you. This book gives you good language. Who'll buy my good language?

Kevel-head, lugger, oakum, pazaree, pintle, poop, plug, prick.

Who'll buy my language. Yes, ma'am? A book for yourself!

Research Notes

During the nineteenth century, innumerable dictionaries were sold to sailors and intending sailors. For example, Richard Henry Dana, who had become famous for his *Two Years Before the Mast*, included an extensive 'Dictionary of Sea Terms' in his *Seaman's Friend*, which went through several editions after its publication in 1851. In such pages the professional argot of mariners was explained:

ARM: The extremity of a yard. Also, the lower part of an anchor, crossing the shank and terminating in the flukes.

APRON: A piece of timber fixed to the lower part of the stern.

BILGE: That part of the floor of a ship upon which she would rest if aground; being the part near the keel which is more in a horizontal than a perpendicular line.

SINGLE SPANISH BURTON: A tackle with three single blocks, or two single blocks and a hook in the bight of one of the running parts.

DOG-VANE: A small vane, made of feathers or buntin, to show the direction of the wind.

DRABLER: A piece of canvass laced to the bonnet of a sail, to give it more drop.

GLUT: A piece of canvass sewed into the centre of a sail near the head. It has an eyelet-hole in the middle for the bunt-jigger or becket to go through.

GUDGEON: A socket in which a rudder rides and pivots.

GOOSENECK: An iron ring fitted to the end of a yard or boom, for various purposes.

GROMMET: A ring formed of rope, by laying round a single strand.

KEVEL-HEAD: Timber heads, bolted to a stanchion, for the belaying of large ropes.

LUGGER: A small vessel carrying lug-sails, which are bent to a yard hanging obliquely to a mast.

PAZAREE: A rope attached to the clew of the foresail and rove through a block on the swinging boom. Used for guying the clews out when before the wind.

PINTLE: A metal bolt, used for hanging a rudder.

POOP: A deck raised over the after part of the spar deck. A vessel is pooped when the sea breaks over her stern.

PLUG: A piece of wood, fitted into a hole in a vessel or boat, so as to let in or keep out water.

PRICK: A quantity of spunyarn or rope laid close up together.

Many 'dialects' of specialist English language were brought into the southern world by colonialism. There was much haggling over vocabularies, definitions and the grasp of crucial concepts. For instance, the 'eighteenth-century Navy ... lacked even a single word for discipline. The word "discipline" itself was known well enough, but in ordinary usage it bore a sense much nearer to its Latin original [i.e. routines of training] than to its modern English sense. ... If people did try to talk about discipline as it is nowadays understood, they had to resort to clumsy and vague circumlocutions about "subordination" and "authority".'

N. A. M. Rodger, *The Wooden World: An Anatomy of the Georgian Navy*, Annapolis, Maryland: Naval Institute Press, 1986, p. 205.

LET US PRAY

Trade Object: Ecclesiastical candle
Storyteller: A small girl reading at a family ceremony of devotion

GIRL: *The Gospel according to Luke. Chapter 21.*[1] *There shall be signs in the sun and in the moon, and in the stars. And in the earth the people shall be at their wits' end. The sea and the water shall be roaring, and men's hearts shall fail them for fear, and for looking after those things which are coming on to the earth.*[2] *Yes, the powers of heaven shall move through the people on earth.*

When these things come to pass, then look up, and lift up your heads, for a reckoning draweth nigh.[3]

Research Notes

'Above all the Places in the world this is the most terrible for thunder and lightening – there has not a day gone over our heads but ther has been Seveer thunder and Lighting –'

Paul G. Fidlon and R. J. Ryan (eds), *The Journal and Letters of Lt. Ralph Clark 1787-1792*, Sydney: Australian Documents Library, 1981, p. 96.

'But for the Faces of the Sky, they are so many, that many of them want proper Names; and therefore it will be convenient to agree upon some determinate ones, by which the most usual may be in brief exprest. As let Cleere signify a very cleere Sky without any Clouds or Exhalations; Checker'd a cleere Sky, with many great white round Clouds, such as are very usual in Summer. Hazy, a Sky that looks whitish, by Reason of the Thickness of the higher parts of the Air, by some Exhalation not formed into Clouds. Thick, a Sky more whitened by a greater Company of Vapours: these do usually make the Luminaries look bearded or hairy, and are oftentimes the Cause of Rings and Haloes about the Sun as well as the Moon. Overcast, when the Vapours so whiten and thicken the Air, that the Sun cannot break through; and of this there are many degrees, which may be exprest by a little, much, more, very much overcast, &c. Let Hairy signify a Sky that hath many small, thin and high Exhalations, which resemble locks of hair, or flakes of Hemp or Flax: whose Varieties may be exprest by straight or curv'd, &c. according to the resemblance they bear. Let Water'd signify a Sky that has many high, thin and small Clouds, looking almost like water'd Tabby, called in some places a Mackeril Sky ... There may be also several faces of the Sky compounded of two or more of these, which may be intelligibly enough exprest by two or more of these Names.'

Robert Hooke, 'A Method for Making a History of the Weather', in Thomas Sprat, *The History of the Royal Society*, London: J. Martyn, 1667, pp. 176 - 78.

1. As in the American colonies, the *Book of Common Prayer* was vital counsel and consolation for many Australian settlers who looked to

the book and to the seasons, the skies, the rivers and 'the beasts of the fields', hoping to recognise signs of providence and righteous purpose directing their colony.

2. 'For THUNDER is the voice of God direct in verse and musick.
For LIGHTNING is a glance of the glory of God.
For the Brimstone that is found at the times of thunder & lightning is worked up by the Adversary.
For the voice is always for infinite good which he strives to impede.
For the Devil can work coals into shapes to afflict the minds of those that will not pray.'

Christopher Smart, *Rejoice in the Lamb*, 1761, quoted in Humphrey Jennings, *Pandaemonium 1660-1886: The coming of the machine as seen by contemporary observers*, London: Picador, 1987, p. 59.

3. 'There has been a great deal of Thunder lightning & heavy rain since our first Arrival here / on the night of the 6th Several trees were shivered with Lightning.'

Newton Fowell, *The Sirius Letters: The Complete Letters of Newton Fowell Midshipman and Lieutenant Aboard the Sirius Flagship of the First Fleet on its Voyage to New South Wales*, edited by Nance Irvine, Sydney: The Fairfax Library, 1988, p. 73.

See also Roy Porter, *The Making of Geology: Earth Science and Britain 1660 -1815*, Cambridge: Cambridge University Press, 1977.

THE AIRE OF MALBROOKE

Trade Object: Tin whistle
Storyteller: A marine playing a tune

MARINE: *On the way out to Botany Bay, Mr Phillip made me play this. Everyday he made me play it. He whistled it for me. The 'Aire of Malbrooke'. I remember it from the dockyards. When I was a boy. It was the favourite of sailors come home from the Americas. The old hands told me it was the song for all people. They said savages the world over, they grow affable when they hear it. Africans. Americans. Brazilians. Javamen. And surely it would pacify the Botany Bay savages also. This was Mr Phillip's opinion.*

What I remember is they laughed out loud. The black people. In the first week we were with them. In the months that followed, they changed their comportment.

[The sailor sings the aire.]*

Ye generals all and champions bold,
Who take delight in the field,
That knock down palaces and castle walls,
But who to death must yield;
Lo! I must go and face that foe,
Without my sword and shield,
I always fought with merry men,
But now to death must yield.

I am an Englishman by birth,
And Malbrooke is my name,
In Devonshire I drew my breath,
That place of noted fame;
I was beloved by all my men,
By King and Prince likewise,
Though many towns I often took,
I did the world surprise.

King Charles the Second I did serve,
To face our foes in France,
And at the field of Ramilies,
We boldly did advance;
The sun was down, the moon did shine,
So loudly I did cry –
'Fight on, my boys, for fair England,
We'll conquer or we'll die.'

And when we gained the victory,
And bravely kept the field,
We took a host of prisoners,
And forced them to yield,
That very day my horse was shot,
All by a musket ball,
As I was mounting up again,
My aide-de-camp did fall.

Now on a bed of sickness prone,
I am resigned to die;
Yet, generals and champions bold,
Stand firm as well as I;

Unto your colours stand you true,
And fight with courage bold,
I have led my men through fire and smoke,
But ne'er was bribed with gold.

*See William Alexander Barratt, *English Folk-Songs collected, arranged and provided with symphonies and accompaniments for the pianoforte*, Darby: Norwood, 1973.

Research Notes

Late January, 1788, at Botany Bay ... 'Between this and our departure [to relocate at Port Jackson] we had several more interviews with the natives, which ended in so friendly a manner, that we began to entertain strong hopes of bringing about a connection with them. Our first object was to win their affections, and our next to convince them of the superiority we possessed: for without the latter, the former we knew would be of little importance. An officer one day prevailed on one of them to place a target, made of bark, against a tree, which he fired at with a pistol, at the distance of some paces. The Indians, though terrified at the report, did not run away, but their astonishment exceeded their alarm, on looking at the shield which the ball had perforated. As this produced a little shyness, the officer, to dissipate their fears and remove their jealousy, whistled the air of Malbrooke, which they appeared highly charmed with, and imitated him with equal pleasure and readiness. I cannot help remarking here, what I was afterwards told by Monsieur De Perrouse, that the natives of California, and throughout all the islands of the Pacific Ocean, and in short wherever he had been, seemed equally touched and delighted with this little plaintive air.

Watkin Tench, *A Narrative of the Expedition to Botany Bay*, first published 1789, reprinted in Watkin Tench, *Sydney's First Four Years*, Sydney: Angus and Robertson, 1961, p. 37.

Music was understood to be integral to the military procedures of colonialism. Noise ordered into useful patterns was both an analogy and an everyday prompt for the work of invasion and settlement. When the New South Wales Corps was commissioned in June 1789, music was written into the structure of law enforcement. Major Francis Grose received a warrant from His Majesty's Government to raise four companies. Each company was to be comprised of 1 Captain, 1 Lieutenant, 1 Ensign, 3 Sergeants, 3 Corporals, 67 Privates and 2 Drummers.

See Ross Fitzgerald and Mark Hearn, *Bligh, Macarthur and the Rum Rebellion*, Sydney: Kangaroo Press, 1988, p. 22.

'Music and dancing were a part of life in wardroom and mess throughout the navy ... ... Some ships had bands of a sort, and privateers, for recruiting purposes, went out of their way to provide music.'

N.A.M. Rodger, *The Wooden World: An Anatomy of the Georgian Navy*, Annapolis, Maryland: Naval Institute Press, 1986, p. 44.

LIKE A KNIFE ON A FINE CHINA PLATE

Trade object: A setting of silver cutlery
Storyteller: A young French woman

WOMAN: *We had been in Sydney only one night. Sleeping in a bed! This is luxury the first time for months after the bunks of a sailing ship. We are on patrols of science, my husband and I. Our occupation, it is to look for the weather, its reasons and decisions. Therefore, this first night on steady ground, we sleep like we have waited for months, in linen which smells like springtime. We sleep down so deep that we are not aware that a man of some kind enters our house and takes away all our silverware – knives and forks which he will sell to the ruffians.*

This puts us in sadness. We have seen all manner of passion. Dark men and women walking naked. Dances in jungle clearings. Our own sailors behaving oddly when we cross the equator. We have known the secrets that love keeps in order to blossom. (I explain this: I dressed like a boy to come on the ship with my husband. For the first week at sea we have romance where I am a boy.[1] *This is unusual. But we do not find it disturbing.) So I have seen things. Metals rusting like sadness in the face of a glacier. Sharks eating their hind quarters in blood's great excitement. Strange things all of these, but we have not been distressed by them.*

And now, when we are in a city with churches and clocks, some unauthorised man makes off with our goods while we are recuperating. This is distressing.[2] *Your Governor, he thinks the*

same way. Governor Macquarie. He is in great distressment. He offers to compensate. What can we say? We have been not treated cordially. By the intruder I mean. And we need to feel well again. So we say thank-you, and the Governor he brings things in exchange for our silver. He brings a dozen fine-woolled sheep, two goats, a cow and a calf. He brings eight black swans and three of your emus. They walk upon the decks like they are on vacation. The emus, their feet go click, click, like knife and fork on fine china. I find this amusing. That they are replacement for cutlery.

So, we feel compensation. The ladies and gentlemen of Sydney amuse us with functions. And there is friendly departure when we sail away to South America, where they have so much weather.[3]

The emus on the deck. Click click at the albatrosses. They all look at each other, emu and albatross, this is to say such as, 'Where do you come from?'

We are in seas large as mountains around the Cape Horn. We come too near to islands called British, the Falklands. There is a rock in our timber. There is water pulling us under. Our men pumping water, singing one song for five hours. The black swans fly to danger in the ocean because they know they are in danger on the ship. I see the black swans drown in cold water. I see the emus scratch at our decking because they run away from the water. They make two noises. One with their breathing. And one with their footing. Both noises like metal on metal. They scream at the water.

We are in the boats when I see three snakes standing on their tails in the water. But I mean the snakes are the emus with their heads up looking for warm sand and salvation. Out here, where there is ice in the water.

I find this distressing. Our silverware disappears a second time.

Research Notes

1. In September, 1817, the corvette *Uranie* sailed from Toulon on a voyage to the Pacific. The Captain was Louis de Freycinet, who had been involved in previous voyages to the south seas, particularly those of Baudin. Accompanying de Freycinet was a 'cabin boy' said to be the son of a friend. Within a few days, this 'boy' admitted to being Louis' wife Rose; the couple had worked the ruse so as not to be separated for the duration of such a major tour of duty. Rose and Louis had been disturbed by the story of Matthew Flinders' separation from his London-bound wife, and they were determined not to undergo a similar marital exile. The crew of the *Uranie* appear to have been delighted by the new member of their party.

See Marnie Bassett, *Realms and Islands: The World Voyage of Rose de Freycinet in the Corvette Uranie 1817-1820*, London: Oxford University Press, 1962, p. 3.

2. The robbery of the de Freycinet's caused scandal and embarrassment in Sydney. The local gentry rallied with gifts to lessen the shame. The ship sailed away on Christmas day Almost certainly, every gift was lost just a few weeks later when the Uranie ran aground near the Falkland Islands.

See Shirley Fenton Huie, *Tiger Lilies: Women Adventurers in the South Pacific*, Sydney: Angus & Robertson, 1990, p. 36.

3. The trip 'was to last over three years and take them around the world. It was not so much a voyage of discovery as a scientific expedition to observe magnetic and meteorological phenomena, perform experiments related to air pressure, take temperatures of the sea at various depths, and observe the customs, products and languages of the native peoples.'

Shirley Fenton Huie, *Tiger Lilies: Women Adventurers in the South Pacific*, Sydney: Angus & Robertson, 1990, p. 24.

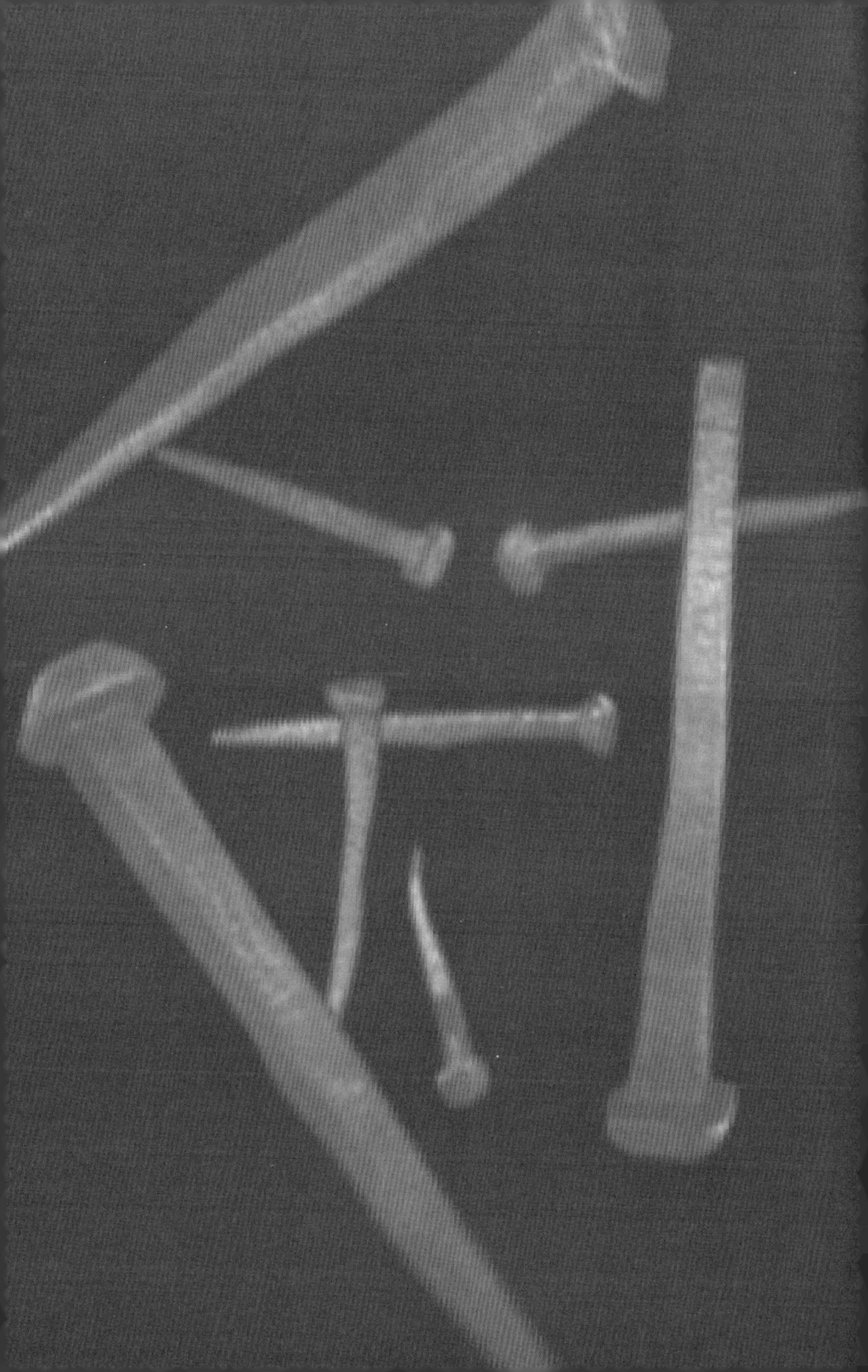

MAD FOR THE USE OF A BODY

Trade Object: Large copper nails
Storyteller: A young Hawaiian woman

WOMAN: *They told us these things were for holding the ship together. They called them 'nails'. But in those strange days, everything had more than one meaning. We could use these things for coconuts. Or for killing a man. For catching a fish. For making a canoe.*

How did we get them from the white men? Well that was the women's job.[1]

We have never seen men more mad for a woman's body. The sailing ships would come to Hawaii, the way they have come for a lifetime now, and the men would be mad for the body of a woman. We made rules for them. The more useful the nail, the more pleasures they could take from us. These were rules to agree upon, but once they got their blood up, the white men never behaved wisely. With their blood up like that, they could be made to give more than the prices we'd agreed upon.

One ship came in from the cold part of the world, where they had been chasing the whale. They were heading home now for Sydney Town. Mostly they were white men. And some men from the islands. And a man calling himself 'Gnunga-Gnunga'.[2] *Black like the ash of a fire. From New South Wales. And him wanting the warm of the sun after where they had been, in the white part of the world. Gnunga-Gnunga. Him looking different from the English men and the Americans. But him wanting for the same*

thing, and getting it, you know, for the price of two long nails. Such was our bargain.

What happens on those ships that makes a man so hungry like that? What is happening in their spirit that makes them pull their canoes apart like that?

Research Notes

1. 'During the nineteenth century, islanders and Europeans met on the beach, exchanged valuable products, offered their labour in each other's service and adopted each other's dress, food, clothing, customs and beliefs. Some travelled widely through strange new lands and waters and created new communities and settlements.'

Max Quanchi and Ron Adams (eds), *Culture Contact in the Pacific: Essays on Contact, Encounter and Response*, Cambridge: Cambridge University Press, 1993, p. 57.

2. '[July, 1793] On the first of this month the *Daedalus* sailed to convey to Captain Vancouver the provisions and stores which had been required by that officer. Lieutenant Hanson, the naval agent on board, received the most pointed orders for the ship to return to this port immediately after having executed the service on which she was then going. ... On board the *Daedalus* also was embarked a native of this country, who was sent by the lieutenant-governor for the purpose of acquiring our language. Lieutenant Hanson was directed by no means to leave him at Nootka, but, if he survived the voyage, to bring him back safe to his friends and countrymen. His native names were Gnung-a gnunga-a, Mur-re-mur-gan; but he had for a long time entirely lost them, even among his own people, who called him "Collins," after the judge-advocate, whose name he had adopted on the first day of his coming among us.'

David Collins, *An Account of the English Colony in New South Wales*, London: Cadell and Davies, 1798, Vol. I, pp. 298 - 99.

Between 1792 and 1794 the storeship HMS *Daedalus*, with Lieutenant James Hanson in command, plied a route from England to Northwest America then to Sydney and back up to Captain Vancouver's settlement at Nootka Sound on the northwest coast of Canada. In transit the ship stopped at New Zealand, Norfolk Island and several other Pacific islands, including Hawaii.

See Ian Hawkins Nicholson, *The Log of Logs: a catalogue of logs, journals, shipboard diaries, letters, and all forms of voyage narratives, for Australia and New Zealand, and surrounding oceans*, 2 vols, Yarooma: Australian Association for Maritime History, 1990 - 93, Vol. I, p. 135.

'[Gnunga-Gnunga] did not appear to have acquired much of our language during his excursion; but seemed to comprehend a great deal more than he could find words to express.'

David Collins, *An Account of the English Colony in New South Wales*, London: Cadell and Davies, 1798, Vol. I, pp. 361 -62.

See also, Kame 'eleihiwa Lilikala, *Native Land and Foreign Desires*, Honolulu: Bishop Museum Press, 1992.

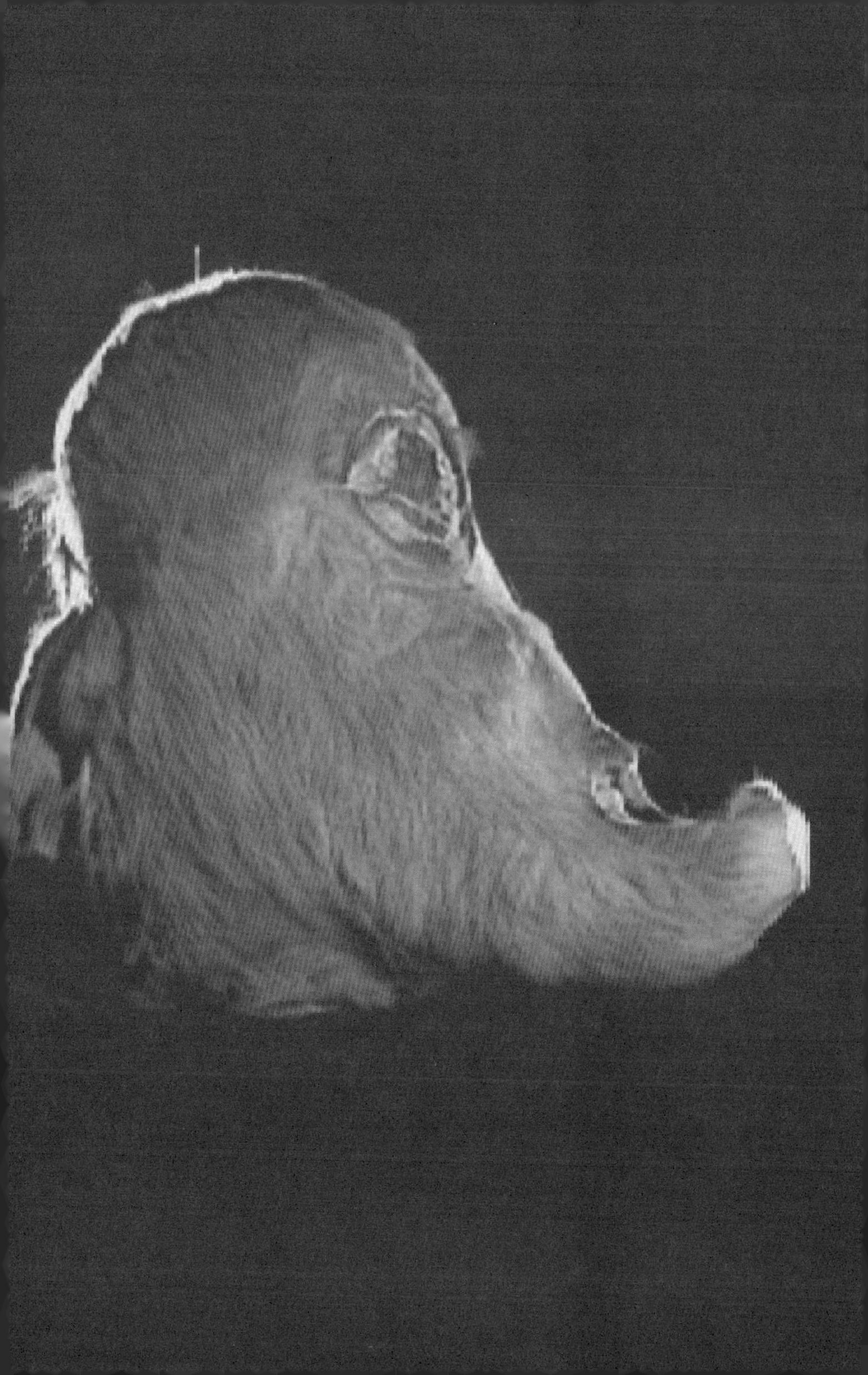

MR MACLEAY'S BUNYIP

Trade Object: A taxidermist's reconstruction of a mutant horse skull
Storyteller: An elderly Englishman, a taxidermist

TAXIDERMIST: *Mr Macleay is perhaps our greatest collector. Of Australian specimens and curiosities. He is building a great museum here in this great museum of a country. I would count it a privilege to be in his employ. To be his taxidermist.*

Imagine my wonder when he tells me of the bunyip. A shepherd has brought its skull to us, found floating in one of our rivers that run inland. This is the animal we have been wishing to find. It is the thing, this bunyip, which haunts all the colony's curious people. Yet we know so little about it. How it hides from the light of day. How it is dangerous most at midnight. That it has noise and smell but is difficult to see. And now we know this much more: the bunyip is killed by water. For here it is, the only specimen we have, dead because it has fallen in a river. Slowly we are making our advances, through the disciplines of science.

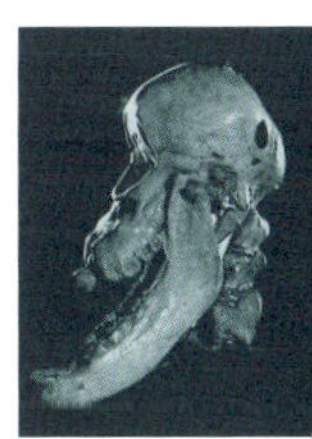

Now, unkind critics say this is nothing more than a horse, with the devil perverting his birth. But I say that's exactly what the bunyip is – the devil perverting all birth. And who's to say the bunyip does not exist when we know how the devil is everywhere in this colony?

If only we could capture a bunyip dry and alive. What a boon it would be, for science and commerce, to have the devil trapped there in warm flesh and breathing in front of you.

Tell me, wouldn't you pay to see such a thing?

Research Notes

'W. S. Macleay issued few publications after his arrival in Sydney. One which shows his interest in the variety of forms in nature was prompted by the discovery of the remains of a supposed bunyip. He had been asked to comment on an incomplete skull which had been found on the lower Murrumbidgee River in 1846. He noted that the cranium was not a fossil, as parts of the membranes and ligaments were still attached. The anatomy of the skull was remarkable. "On first inspection it seems very anomalous, differing from the skulls of all known Mammalia, and gives us the notion of some bird such as the Emu or Ostrich; which is owing to the breadth between the eye-orbits, which are close to the molars of the upper jaw, and also owing to the great development of occiput." The animal was young, possibly a foetus. The teeth were like those of a horse. ... Macleay had in his possession another unusual skull, that of the foetus of a mare which had been found floating in the Hawkesbury River in 1841. (The skull and prepared skin are still in the Macleay Museum.)'

Peter Stanbury and Julian Holland (eds), *Mr Macleay's Celebrated Cabinet: the history of the Macleays and their museum*, Sydney: University of Sydney Macleay Museum, 1988, p. 33.

NO SWINE IN SYDNEY'S BUSHLAND

Trade Object: A salted pig's head in a barrel of brine
Storyteller: A young marine in uniform

MARINE: *We were here only a couple of weeks and the Governor picks me out of a line-up and says he's got a job for me. 'Why me?' I ask myself. And he answers like I spoke it out loud (which I still worry I did). He says, 'You, because I'm told you were a farmhand'. Which I was, before I went down to London and joined with the boys. So he says, 'You'd know about pigs.' And I think to myself, 'Oooh, hold your smart tongue.' And he says, 'I mean pigs with the curl in the tail.' And I think again, 'Did I say something?' Or is that what makes a fellow a leader? Knowing what another man's thinking. Like his mind is pages with words on 'em. Is reading what makes a man a captain?*

Anyways, the Governor he says, 'I want you take a dozen pigs ... out there ... I want you to take them out there and make sure they're happy. I want you to take them out there and stay with them two or three days until they tell you they're happy.' 'You know about pigs,' he says, 'so they'll tell you when they're happy.'

What he's got in his mind is this plan to have pigs everywhere in the country.[1] *Like in Tahiti, he says. Where they're everywhere now and nobody goes hungry. I want to say to him does he know how a pig can eat up the country when it runs in a place without fences. But I mustn't have said it, because the next day, I'm driving a cartload of pigs out into the bush.*

The horse is skittish. She's rolling her eyes and jacking down on the ground. I'm whipping her so she snorts and bucks forward and all the pigs in the tray tumble over and squeal out their snouts so I have to turn and yell at them to quieten down, the little piggies. And then the horse does its jig again, and I'm yellin' and whippin' again. And we go like this into the trees. Like we're all one engine designed by God only for making noise.[2] *This takes a half of the day.*

At last, I stop and let the tailboard down. The pigs take off with noise like the devil. And then it's quiet like heaven. For a minute or two. Till I hear crackle and fizz. I hear a fire coming at me. Three sides it's coming at me. No, four sides. It's all around me. I scream out with my fright. Then the pigs come back with two times their noise. And they see what I see, that it's all around us. What more can they do? They make four times the noise. It's all they can do, is make noise. So the horse makes its neigh also, to add to the pigs. Then we all breathe at once and every creature is quietly showing the white in its eye.

But straightaway, well, the noise machine is back on again. Because, now I see the black men running on the other side of the fire.[3] *And it's like they're writing a message for me: 'you white fellows are one thing ... but the pigs ... we say no to the pigs.'*

What can I do? I cut the horse free from the cart and jump on her back. And we ride screaming through the flames.

I go direct to see the Governor. I'm looking like a black man. He can see I don't deserve punishing.

So. Two weeks later. The Governor, he comes to my tent and says, 'Go do that again, with the pigs.' I say out loud, 'You mean with the pigs and the noise.' He looks at me like he's saying 'Did you go mad there in the flames?' He doesn't say it out loud. But

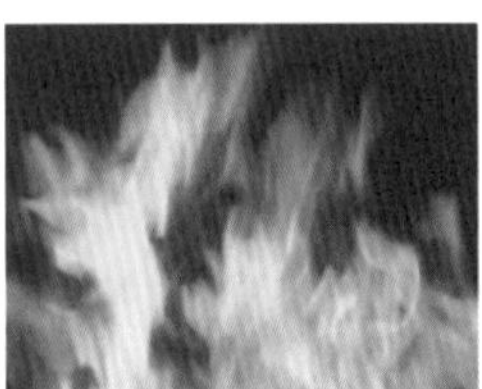

it's like he's words on a page and suddenly I can read him. It occurs to me, if I do this the right way, I must be a captain soon. Because I can read the man now, you know.

So I get back on the noise machine. And it's the same day exactly. Horse and pigs the same, fire the same, and the black men writing NO with their firesticks. I think I can read this much. I think like, they're out there writing for me.

I come back and tell the Governor. I tell him, that's the end of the pigs. I tell him it was a good idea when he thought it but it is not a good idea now.

He reckons me right in this way of thinking. He reckons me right. So I'm waiting for an officer's coat soon. A fine red coat. They eat so much better than I do, the men with the coats. I want to wear a red coat. Even if they don't get to eat much fresh pig. The officers, I mean. It's mostly salted swine that comes in barrels from Tahiti. That's what they eat.

Research Notes

1. Letter from Governor Arthur Phillip to Lord Sydney, February 12, 1790 ... 'My intentions of turning swine into the woods to breed have been prevented by the natives so frequently setting fire to the country.'

Historical Records of Australia, 1790, p. 142.

2. 'That the Soul of Brutes is material, and the whole Animal, Soul and Body, but a mere Machine, is the Opinion publickly own'd and declar'd of Des Cartes, Gassendus, Dr Willis and others. ... This Opinion, I say, I can hardly digest. I should rather think Animals to be endu'd with a lower Degree of Reason, than that they are meer Machines.'

John Ray, 'The Wisdom of God', 1691, quoted in Humphrey Jennings, *Pandaemonium 1660-1886: The coming of the machine as seen by contemporary observers*, London: Picador, 1987, p. 22.

3. Firing the country was almost certainly a customary procedure in the Sydney region, but it is also clear that Aboriginal people used fire as a weapon to stall the advance of the strangers. For as long as the white people stayed in the Eora region, the black people studied them. By early 1791, Watkin Tench was noting how Aborigines all the way out to Richmond were thoroughly informed of the manners of the newcomers: 'The ease with which these people behaved among strangers, was as conspicuous, as unexpected. They seated themselves at our fire, partook of our biscuit and pork, drank from our canteens, and heard our guns going off around them, without betraying any symptom of fear, distrust, or surprize.'

Watkin Tench, *A Complete Account of the Settlement at Port Jackson*, first published in 1793, and reprinted in *Sydney's First Four Years*, Sydney: Angus & Robertson, 1961, p. 230.

NOTHING IS WASTED

Trade Object: A large liquor barrel
Storyteller: An Irish tavern-maid

MAID: *At closing time, there's the barrels. The barrels we've emptied in the day. Well somebody's got to clean them. Your man, he's got a scheme. The blackfellas do the barrels for him. The way it started, he'd give them a nip. Of rum in a bottle, I mean. Cheap enough payment, for the work they do.*

But how cunning is this? These days, he lets them keep the water they use for the washing. The more they scrub with it, the more strong the water. They drain it out of the barrel and drink it. A blackfella does two barrels and he's legless, that's if he's cleaned them well. How cunning is this? These days, your man doesn't even pay with rum in a bottle.

Is this the right way to go about things? Don't ask me such questions. If the blacks weren't doing the scrubbing, who do you think it'd be, with her arse sticking out of a barrel?

Research Notes

At Botany Bay on January 20th, 1788, Philip Gidley King used alcohol to extricate himself from what he perceived to be an anxious situation when the Bay people were gathering around his row-boat: 'we made them a few more presents, but found it necessary to put a stop to our generosity as they were increasing fast in numbers & having only a boats crew with me I was apprehensive that they might find means to surprize us as every one of them were armed with lances, and short bludgeons – I gave two of them a glass of Wine which they had no sooner tasted than they spit it out ...' This may have been the first incident in a bleak history of alcohol and Aboriginal experience.

Philip Gidley King, *The Journal of Philip Gidley King: Lieutenant, RN 1787-1790* (edited by Paul G. Fidlon and R. J. Ryan), Sydney: Australian Documents Library, 1980, p. 35.

The Russian scientist, F. G. Bellingshausen, who visited Sydney in 1820, noted how alcohol had become fundamental to transactions between whites and blacks in the colony. He observed that 'the tavern-keepers mostly hire natives to rinse out their spirit casks. The first wash, which has a fairly strong flavour of spirits, they call "bull", and the natives take this as payment for their labour. They pour it into a vessel and, when the work is done, drink it until intoxicated. Although this has been prohibited the tavern proprietors find it a convenient way of paying natives for various sorts of work and continue to ignore the prohibition.'

F. G. Bellingshausen, quoted in Glynn Barratt, *The Russians at Port Jackson 1814–1822*, Canberra: Australian Institute of Aboriginal Studies, 1981.

To similar effect, in Central Queensland during the 1880s, English station-managers and Chinese merchants procured Aboriginal labour and/or passivity by plying local tribes with the ash left over from opium pipes after the moneyed clients had finished with the drug.

See Carl Lumholtz, *An Account of Four Years' Travels in Australia and of Camp Life with the Aborigines of Queensland*, New York: Charles Scribner's Sons, 1889, p. 338.

THE

SYDNEY  GAZETTE,

And New South Wales Advertiser.

PUBLISHED BY AUTHORITY.

Vol. I. SATURDAY, MARCH 5, 1803. Number 1.

It is hereby ordered, that all Advertisements, Orders, &c. which appear under the Official Signature of the Secretary of this Colony, or of any other Officer of Government, properly authorised to publish them in the SYDNEY GAZETTE, AND NEW SOUTH WALES ADVERTISER, are meant, and must be deemed to convey official and sufficient Notifications, in the same Manner as if they were particularly specified to any ONE Individual, or Others, to whom such may have a Reference.

By Command of His Excellency the Governor and Commander in Chief, WILLIAM NEATE CHAPMAN, Secretary.

Sydney, March 5th, 1803.

General Orders.

REPEATED Complaints having been made of the great losses sustained by the Settlers at Hawkesbury, from the vexatious conduct of the Boatmen by whom they send their Grain to Sydney, the following Regulations are to be observed.

Every person sending grain from the Hawkesbury to Sydney in an open boat, or a boat that is not trust-worthy, the Magistrates are directed to take no notice thereof.

If on proof it appears that the Master of a Boat receives more grain than the vessel ought to take with safety, the Master shall make good any quantity he may throw overboard, or otherwise damage, lose the freight of that part, and, on conviction before two Magistrates, forfeit 5l. to the Orphan Fund.

If it shall appear to the Magistrates that grain coming round to Sydney has been wetted, that it might weigh heavier or measure more than the quantity put on board, the Master will, on conviction, forfeit 5l. to the Orphan Fund.

The Commanding Officer of the New South Wales Corps will direct the Corporal of the Guard on board the Castle of Good Hope to read the General Orders that are marked off in the Extracts he is furnished with, to the Corporal, and the Party that relieves him; the said Orders are also to be read to the Guard on board the Supply Hulk.

By Command of His Excellency W. N. CHAPMAN, Sec.
Government House, Feb. 21, 1803.

THE Receiving Granaries at Parramatta and Hawkesbury, being filled with Wheat which is spoiling, no more can be taken in at those places until further Orders, except in payment for Government Debts, and the Whalers Investments lodged in the Public Stores.

Wheat will continue to be received into the Stores at Sydney, until further Orders.

Wheat will be issued to the Civil, Military, &c. until further Orders; except to the detachments and labouring people at Castle-Hill, Seven-Hills, and other Out Posts, who will receive Flour, as they have not the convenience of Mills.

By Command, &c. W. N. CHAPMAN, Sec
Government House, Feb. 24, 1803.

THE GOVERNOR having permitted Mr. Robert Campbell to land 4000 Gallons of Spirits for the domestic use of the Inhabitants, from the Castle of Good Hope, it will be divided in the following proportion, viz.

For the Officers on the Civil Establishment, (including Superintendants and Storekeepers), 1000 Gallons;

For Naval and Military Commissioned Officers, 1000 Gallons;

For the Licensed People, 1000 Gallons;

To be distributed to such Persons as the GOVERNOR may think proper to grant Permits to, 1000 Gallons.

The above to include the Civil and Military Officers at Norfolk Island.

By Command, &c. W. N. CHAPMAN, Sec.
Government House, March 4, 1803.

ADDRESS.

Innumerable as the Obstacles were which threatened to oppose our Undertaking, yet we are happy to affirm that they were not insurmountable, however difficult the task before us.

The utility of a PAPER in the COLONY, as it must open a source of solid information, will, we hope, be universally felt and acknowledged. We have courted the assistance of the INGENIOUS and INTELLIGENT :--- We open no channel to Political Discussion, or Personal Animadversion :---Information is our only Purpose; that accomplished, we shall consider that we have done our duty in an exertion to merit the Approbation of the PUBLIC, and to secure a liberal Patronage to the SYDNEY GAZETTE.

ON THIS DAY

Trade Object: Piles of newspapers and journals

Storyteller: A bourgeois woman, at the breakfast table, browses from an array of newspapers and magazines – *Australian, Monitor, Colonist, Australian Chronicle*

WOMAN: *On this day May 4, 1832, it is calculated that during the foregoing fortnight, there entered Port Jackson, twenty-nine coasting vessels and there departed twenty-seven other vessels. This computation does not include the various departures and arrivals from abroad.*

June 4, 1842. The whaling vessel Waterwitch *on the twenty-third of March this year of 1842 did put in at Lord Howe's Island for refreshments. The Captain and a boat's crew went ashore for the things they stood in need of, some of which were sent on board that evening, and directions were sent by the Captain, who remained ashore, to send all boats at daylight for the remainder. In the night, however, the vessel put to sea, and after waiting some days, the Commander was obliged to give her up. The remainder of the crew having, it is supposed, carried her off with the intention of disposing of her and her cargo at some foreign port.*

September 5, 1828 ... Seal skins are in brisk demand, as also sperm oil, both at high prices. ... 4th June, 1831 ... Black whale oil has become very scarce, every available gallon having been shipped for the English markets.

November 3, 1838 ... W. E. Browne, many years in the Honorable East India Company's service, and now agent at Calcutta, will undertake to procure Hill Coolies for any parties requiring them, to be landed at Port Phillip or Sydney at the same comparative rates as he has already sent them to Mauritius.

December 1, 1836 ... Mr Denton, the poulterer, has returned to this colony by the vessel Florentia *and has brought with him a great variety of very beautiful fancy pigeons, consisting of dragons, carriers, tumblers, pouters, fantails and so on and a pair of small song thrushes. ... By the same vessel, a number of shepherds have arrived for Messrs. Campbell and Co. They are accompanied by about a dozen and a half of real English sheep dogs. These will provide a valuable importation to sheep owners.*

October 4, 1827 ... Mr Earle is at present engaged in painting a comprehensive view of Sydney, from the North Shore, for a nobleman in England.

November 30, 1837 ... For sale now in Mr Campbell's store ... live birds of all kinds from Australia's interior. Recently arrived from collecting expedition on western plains. Wholesale prices for retailers, at home and abroad.

LOOK UPON MY WORKS, YE MIGHTY, AND DESPAIR

Trade Object: A small anthology of poems
Storyteller: An Irish convict man

CONVICT: *Sure, how can you think well in this place? Not to mind the ants and the heat and such, how can you think when it is forbidden to talk in your language?*[1] *And what is there to read? Only things in English language. You must know how those words are sand in the mouth.*

But even in the darkest night there is a glimmer of moonlight. I am told that new poems have arrived in the Bond Store. New poems by Percy Shelley. If we must read things in English, these are the things.

[He takes up the book and reads 'Ozymandias'.]

I met a traveller from an antique land
Who said: Two vast and trunkless legs of stone
Stand in the desert ... Near them, on the sand,
Half sunk, a shattered visage lies, whose frown,
And wrinkled lip, and sneer of cold command,
Tell that its sculptor well those passions read
Which yet survive, stamped on these lifeless things,
The hand that mocked them, and the heart that fed:
And on the pedestal these words appear:
"My name is Ozymandias, king of kings:
Look on my works, ye Mighty, and despair!"
Nothing beside remains. Round the decay

Of that colossal wreck, boundless and bare
The lone and level sands stretch far away.

[He looks up and proclaims.]

Now, that's a poem!

Research Notes

1. 'Though the literacy rate of Irish males was not markedly different from that of English males (about 60 per cent could read and between 40 and 50 per cent could also write) many of the Irish [in the early years of the New South Wales colony] did not speak English among themselves, but Gaelic.' Officers and marines actively discouraged the utterance of this 'secret' language.

Patrick O'Farrell, *The Irish in Australia*, Sydney: UNSW, 1986, p. 25.

See also, Jakelin Troy, 'Language Contact in Early Colonial New South Wales 1788 to 1791', in Michael Walsh and Colin Yallop, *Language and Culture in Aboriginal Australia*, Canberra: Aboriginal Studies Press, 1993.

The following sonnet by Shelley might also please a republican Irishman.

England in 1819

An old, mad, blind, despised, and dying king –
Princes, the dregs of their dull race, who flow
Through public scorn – mud from a muddy spring –
Rulers who neither see, nor feel, nor know,
Till they drop, blind in blood, without a blow –
A people starved and stabbed in the untilled field –
An army, which liberticide and prey
Makes us a two-edged sword to all who wield –
Golden and sanguine laws which tempt and slay;
Religion, Christless, Godless – a book sealed;
A Senate – Time's worst statute unrepealed –
Are graves, from which a glorious Phantom may
Burst, to illumine our tempestuous day.

SING OF GOD'S GARRISON

Trade Object: Pulpit and ecclesiastical candle
Storyteller: Preacher

PREACHER: *Let us consider the services of the sea, for they are innumerable. The sea is provided by the Almighty as one way to our home up in heaven.*[1] *Let us go down to the sea. It will lead us to the godless places of the world. And there we will please God by setting His fire in the gloomy huts and damp forests. And we shall locate there all the wonders that god has provided us.*

The sea douses meteors in multiform shapes. It sings hosannas in the mouth of great storms. It harbours ill–formed, deformed and unformed things best named here as 'monsters', and there are dark malevolent men most surely amongst these. Yes! In the sea such anomalies are there so we can find them and tame them.

Verily, the South Sea is God's gift to Christian soldiers. Did I say 'soldiers'?! Onward Christian sailors! The sea has provided to us the world's ocean-borne commodities expressly for our use. The sea is the uniter of all the globe's nations. It contains the products of rivers. It delights the eye with diversified colours and rouses the body with unresting motion. It offers great gifts of jewellery that some men call islands. Fiji. Otaheitie. Hawaii. Solomons' Islands. Now according to His Almighty will, these might be mere baubles. Or they might be great shrines in the planetary temple of the Lord.

Gracious God, explain for me your ocean! It pitches and yaws with endless definition.[2] *It is an open field for the merchandise of peace, a turbulent field for the contentions of war. In its depths it*

peace, a turbulent field for the contentions of war. In its depths it delivers diversity for diet plus the matter of wealth and the medicines of health. It has pearls and corals for mouth-gaping wonder. It has amber and ambergris also providing amazement.

What more can it offer us? I have not yet concluded! It carries heartwarming greetings to friends who are distant. It delights and refreshes whenever you are weary. It is a map of knowledge and a mystery past dimension. It is storage for the merchant and customs for government.

Because of the sea, the sky collects clouds. Because of the sea, the air takes sweet breath. Because of the sea, the soil has its suppleness, and the rivers draw tides that lull fish to our nets.

Friends, array this in your mind's eye: each day the sun rises, and the ocean carries one million Englishmen in boats blown by the breath of God's spirit. Rejoice now, my friends, for the sea is undoubted our destiny. In all its transitions, it is our storehouse, our temple and our wall of defence. It is God's undulating garrison in guard of our state.

I will not detain you any longer. It's time now for conclusion.

Consider two questions. Why did God make Great Britain an island?[3] *And why did he send James Cook down amongst us? Ponder this a moment. Now let me offer an answer, the same one for both questions: it is because we are destined in our whiteness to bring light to the dark waters all over God's firmament.*

I'll be leaving you now. May God's peace go along with you.

Research Notes

This sermon is a very 'free adaptation' of *The Commendations of Navigation as an Art*, by Samuel Purchas in his *Purchas His Pilgrimes*, first published 1625, Vol. I, Glasgow: MacLehose, 1905, pp. 46 - 7.

1. 'There is no sea in the Garden of Eden. Within the closed countryside of Paradise, there is no liquid horizon, no great expanse where vision goes to vapour. Wishing to penetrate the mysteries of the ocean is like wishing to penetrate the ineffable nature of divinity.'

Alain Corbin, *Le Territoire du vide: l'occident et le desir du rivage (1750-1840)*, Paris: Aubier, 1988, p. 12. My translation.

2. 'Water is the element best suited to showing how forces combine in the world. Water brings substances together! Even materials as different as sugar and salt – it receives them equally. It impregnates all colours, flavours and odours.'

Gaston Bachelard, *L'Eau et les reves: Essai sur l'imagination de la matiere*, Paris: Librairie Jose Corti, 1942, p. 126. My translation.

3. 'Where should the child of England look but to the sea! The sea is our birthright and inheritance. Nature herself seems to point out to us our proper path and our real interests, by keeping us constantly in sight of the ocean.'

Anon., 'Australian Sperm Whale Fishery', in *The Australian Quarterly Journal of Theology, Literature and Science*, Number 1 (1828), p. 87.

'For the FOUNTAINS and SPRINGS are the life of the waters working up to God.
For they are in SYMPATHY with the waters above the Heavens, which are solid.
For the Fountains, springs and rivers are all of them from the sea, whose water is filtrated and purified by the earth.
For is Water above the visible surface in a spiritualizing state, which

cannot be seen but by the application of a CAPILLARY TUBE.
For the ASCENT of VAPOURS is the return of thanksgiving from all humid bodies.

Christopher Smart, *Rejoice in the Lamb*, 1761, quoted in Humphrey Jennings, *Pandaemonium 1660-1886: The coming of the machine as seen by contemporary observers*, London: Picador, 1987, p. 57.

See also, J. H. Parry, *The Discovery of the Sea*, London: Wiedenfeld and Nicolson, 1975.

See also, W. H. Auden, *The Enchafed Flood, or The Romantic Iconography of the Sea*, New York: Vintage, 1950.

See also, William Lisle Bowles, *The Spirit of Discovery; or, The Conquest of the Ocean*, Bath: Cruttwell, 1804.

SMOKE SMELLS LIKE GOD

Trade Object: Sandalwood incense sticks
Storyteller: A blind merchant sailor

SAILOR: *We crept out of Sydney Town with the darkness around us. On Mr Lord's ship. For gathering sandalwood in the Feejees.[1] Not strictly law-abiding. Because we're not in the East India Company. It's the first years of the new century and we're all set to have a big time. Mr Lord's promises. Haul up at the islands, and then sweep off to China, swap wood for tea, fill up with money, come home, and swagger around! Mr Lord's promises.[2]*

They burn the sandalwood in China to help them think of god. The smoke smells like god.[3] Well, smoke always smells like something.

Yes, I had a big time. Two days out from the Feejees I wake up seeing smoke and red stains in the sky, and as the day gets older the sky gets darker. At midday I look at the sun and it's a soft apricot sitting nice up there saying, 'Look at me forever, am I too hot, no I'm not, I'm softer than lamplight.' True, by now I know something, but I don't want to believe it. Heart's beating like horses' hooves all afternoon. Yes, at sunset I see nothing. In that day I am gone blind.

Still, you know how it might be a dream? You might wake up to the daylight and laugh at your mind? So I go to sleep sweating, thinking maybe I'm already asleep and now I'm going to dream inside a dream. But I wake up the next morning and have to call out for assistance. I can't piss without help.

Now this makes a man desperate. He thinks also he's useless. Day two of blindness – I hear cries about 'land ho', I hear feet running men to see the mountains and forests, I have to ask mates to point me which way to imagine the islands.

So I decide to die on the islands. My friend he doesn't argue. He can't think of me living because he can't see himself living, like if he's in my shoes. I give him my clothes, my gloves. I give him my shoes! He takes me to the sandalwood, where I think I want to die ... you know, in the trees that smell like god.

But how much do we know?! The dark men from Feejee, they take us there and my friend says this is no place to die – the sandalwood trees they look like nothing ... they're like dead things themselves and it's rocky and dry there. The only place on the island ... where it's rocky and dry. I learn in days later that sandalwood it's like this ... the more dry where it grows the more godly the oil that makes the wood smell so.[4]

So I say, 'I don't want to die here ... I want a big place, with big trees and darkness.' The black men, they understand this, and they point my friend to the forest.

Well, now it gets to be mystery.

We go into the forest, and I find it's beautiful there, with all these smells and noises, and a temperature saying 'welcome'. I say this out loud, how there might be good things, still, to encounter in the world. I say this out loud that my friend he might hear me. But he's gone quiet. Like there's terror coming out of him. I can smell him in terror. I can discern such a thing here. You see, I have new skills here. I find I am a gifted man here, in the dark forest.

I find I can live, among the trees, in the dark forest. In the smells and the noises. There are signs for me there. For me, with my new faculties. I find I can live in the world therefore.

So how is this happening! That I want to live now, here, where I have just been intending to die! And my friend is in terror! He tells me later that there was no place to look, that there was nothing like a vista to comfort his eye. And all he had was the invisible noises and the smells coming from nowhere and that this in all ways is terror.

So I have to lead him out of the dark woods. I lead him to the light, and he leads me to the ship. Slowly he can talk again. And we say it's worth it to be alive. Both of us.

I smell sandalwood in the air! My friend says the ship is deserted. I smell god in the air! My friend says the trees are on fire. I hear muskets exploding. Bright parakeets are on fire. I hear the voices of anger in more than one language. I hear the crew of my ship running down to the shoreline. I hear the men of the Feejees throw spears and hard objects. I hear women commence with howling and wailing. I smell foliage burning. I hear gunpowder exploding. And I smell somebody's god in the air.

Aye, in so many ways in these last two days, I am changed.

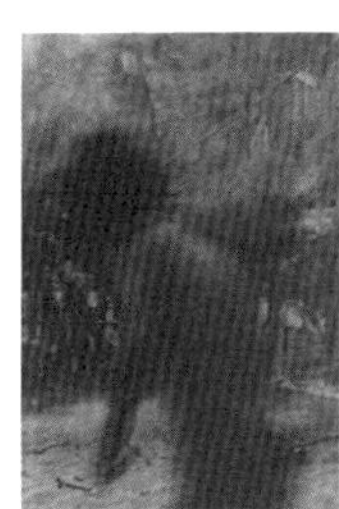

Research Notes

'February 29, 1828 – Arrived at Domineque Island. Sent the boats well armed into Hanhapoowa Bay, to trade.'

Ship-journal of Dr William Dalton, Surgeon to the South Seas whaler, the *Harriet*, in Neil Gunson (ed.) *The Dalton Journal. Two Whaling Voyages to the South Seas 1823-1829*, Canberra: National Library of Australia, 1990, p. 115.

See also, D. R. Hainsworth, *Builders and Adventurers: The Traders and the Emergence of the Colony 1788-1821*, Melbourne: Castle, 1968.

1. 'The collectors of sandal-wood should be encourag'd, as the Americans will certainly obtain every pound of that valuable article which our colonists neglect to procure. Its high price, however, will amply provide for the cost of sending it to England, where the East India Company will find it in their interest to purchase it at rates very advantageous to the original shippers.'

Sir Joseph Banks, 'Some Remarks on the Present State of the Colony of Sidney, in New South Wales, and on the means most likely to render it a productive, instead of an expensive, settlement', June 4, 1806, in F. M. Bladen (ed.), *Historical Records of New South Wales, Vol. VI – King and Bligh. 1806, 1807, 1808*, Sydney: Government Printer, 1898, p. 89.

2. 'By the early nineteenth century emancipist businessmen in New South Wales had interests in land, manufacturing and shipbuilding. They were among the first to send ships to Pacific Islands such as Fiji to obtain sandalwood, for which there was a market. Lord's ship, the *Marcia*, returned from Fiji with the first cargo of sandalwood in 1805.'

Ross Fitzgerald and Mark Hearn, *Bligh, Macarthur and the Rum Rebellion*, Sydney: Kangaroo Press, 1988, pp. 48 - 49.

3. Once Buddhism began to flourish in China, sandalwood was required in great volumes for devotional purposes. Indian Buddhism had been well supplied by local trees, but China had to import supplies. Since the sixth century AD, Persian and Arab merchants had traded sandalwood into China. By the turn of the nineteenth century, Pacific Island supplies were keenly sought.

See Dorothy Shineberg, *They Came for Sandalwood: A Study of the Sandalwood Trade in the South-West Pacific 1830-1865*, Melbourne: Melbourne University Press, 1967, p. 1.

4. Sandalwood trees are variable in their 'yield' of oil. Wood was classified by merchants as 'red', 'yellow' or 'white', in descending order of value. The tree itself is seldom imposing, averaging eight feet in height. The oil is in the heart-wood of the slender grey trunk. The nearer the roots, the greater the quantity of oil. Traders believed that dry and rocky conditions produced the 'red trees'.

See Dorothy Shineberg, *They Came for Sandalwood: A Study of the Sandalwood Trade in the South-West Pacific 1830-1865*, Melbourne: Melbourne University Press, 1967, p. 2.

SOMETHING SO BAD MAKES SOMETHING SO SWEET

Trade Object: Bottle of perfume
Storyteller: A young girl, prompted by questions from a man

GIRL: *This is perfume with the scented water. For ladies. And for gentlemen to give to ladies. But it starts with the men. That's what Wiki told me. He says that the men who catch the big fish put their hands in its belly so they can make perfume.*

MAN: *Who is Wiki?*

GIRL: *Wiki is a brown man. Very big. He's got white teeth. He catches whales and he grew up in the islands. He used to live in a house with legs. We live in a hotel-house. Wiki doesn't go whale-fishing all the time. When he buys a room at our house, that's when he hasn't got a boat to live on.*

MAN: *What were you saying about the perfume?*

GIRL: *It's because of the things it eats. Squids. The whale eats a big squid and it rubs at the whale's belly inside and the belly makes a thing that Wiki calls 'ambergris'.*[1]

MAN: *Ambergris?*

GIRL: *The ambergris sits in the whale's belly and stops the squid's sharp bits. It smells very bad when Wiki pulls it out.*[2] *But that's not so strange is it? The whale is sick and Wiki is not helping. Of course it smells bad.*

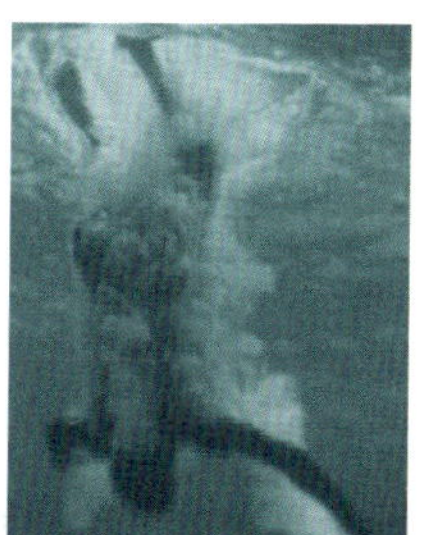

MAN: *Ambergris makes perfume?*[3]

GIRL: *Ambergris makes* perfume*! This is strange. Wiki shakes his head when he says this. He says, 'Is this how the world must work now ... we must make something good out of so much that's gone bad?' He shakes his head when he says this. Well he's right. It is confusing.*

Research Notes

1. 'ambergris n. Waxlike odoriferous substance found floating in tropical seas and in intestines of sperm whale.'

Concise Oxford Dictionary

2. '[The] breath of the whale is frequently attended with such an insupportable smell, as to bring on a disorder of the brain.'

Antonio de Ulloa, *A Voyage to South America, 1758*, as quoted by Herman Melville in the prefatory 'Extracts' to *Moby-Dick*, first published in 1851.

3. '[Ambergris] is also constantly bought by the pilgrims who travel to Mecca, probably to offer it there, and make use of it in fumigations in the same manner as frankincense is used in Catholic countries. The Turks make use of it as an aphrodisiac.'

Thomas Beale, *The Natural History of the Sperm Whale*, London: John Van Voorst, 1839, p. 134.

'At times, when closely pursued, [the sperm whale] will disgorge what are supposed to be the detached arms of the squid; some of them thus exhibited exceeding twenty and thirty feet in length.'

Herman Melville, *Moby-Dick*, first published in 1851, Chapter LIX.

'In truth it turned out to be one of those problematical whales that seem to dry up and die with a sort of prodigious dyspepsia, or indigestion; leaving their defunct bodies almost entirely bankrupt of anything like oil. Nevertheless ... we shall see that no knowing fisherman will ever turn up his nose at such a whale as this ... ... Stubb quickly pulled to the floating body ... Seizing his sharp boat-spade, he commenced an excavation in the body, a little behind the side fin ... ... And all the time numberless fowls were diving, and ducking and screaming, and yelling, and fighting around them. Stubb was beginning to look disappointed, especially as the horrible nosegay increased, when suddenly from out of the very heart of this plague, there stole a faint stream of perfume, which flowed through the tide of bad smells without being absorbed … … … Dropping his spade, he thrust both hands in, and drew out handfuls of something that looked like ripe Windsor soap, or rich mottled old cheese; very unctuous and savoury withal. You might easily dent it with your thumb; it is of a hue between yellow and ash color. And this, good friends, is ambergris, worth a gold guinea an ounce to any druggist.'

Herman Melville, *Moby-Dick*, first published in 1851, Chapter XCI.

'[There] were found in this ambergris, certain hard, round, bony plates, which at first Stubb thought might be sailors' trousers buttons; but it afterwards turned out that they were nothing more than pieces of small squid bones embalmed in that manner.

Herman Melville, *Moby-Dick*, first published in 1851, Chapter XCII.

TELL HIM THINGS

Trade Object: Pen and paper
Storyteller: A young Aboriginal woman

WOMAN: *The fish were dying. The people were dying. The white men were here. What were the stories for them? We didn't know the stories for them.*

'WILLIAM DAWES' – a white man came up to me making noises. 'William Dawes' – that was one of his noises. 'William Dawes.' 'William Dawes.' And he did hand talk, eh.[1] *With his hands.*

So I say my name out loud, to see what he does with it. He makes marks on paper. Every noise I make, he puts black marks down on paper.

The old people, they're talking. They say to me, 'Let him come. Let him come and make noises. Tell him things. Tell him things that are not important.'

Because we needed to know about these men. In those days, we didn't know what they meant to us.

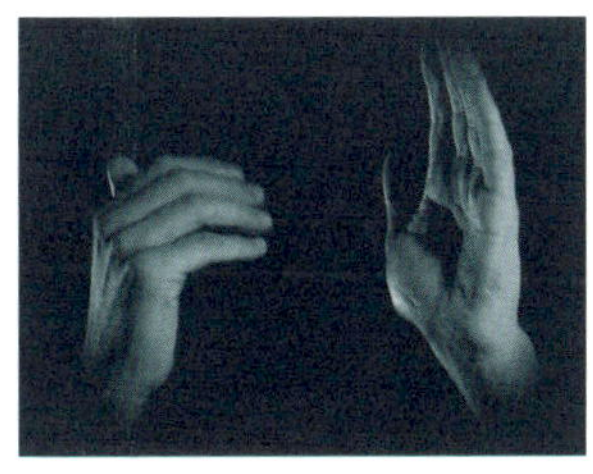

Research Notes

'The most valuable sources of information about the Sydney Language are three manuscripts now held in the School of Oriental and African Studies in London and catalogued as "manuscript 41645 parts a, b and c". Manuscripts "a" and "b" were produced by Lieutenant William Dawes RN, a scientist with the First Fleet. They contain his conversations with a number of Aboriginal people who are familiar from the journals of other First Fleet writers. However, the person most often referred to by Dawes was a young woman, "Patyegarang" or as he usually called her "Patye". Patye taught Dawes her language and he, in return, taught her to speak and read English. Their conversations reveal each exploring the culture of the other with some of the broader issues concerning Aboriginal people being revealed in Patye's comments. For example, Patye told Dawes that the Aboriginal people of the district were angry because the colonists had settled on their land and they were afraid of the colonists' guns.

'Manuscript "c" seems to have been the work of several authors as it is written in at least thee different hands including both "rough" and "fair" scripts.'

Jakelin Troy, *The Sydney Language*, Canberra: Australian Institute of Aboriginal and Torres Strait Islander Studies, 1994, p. 14. Microfilm copies of the Dawes manuscripts are available in the Mitchell Library in Sydney.

Despite the fact that the English relied intensively on their own rudimentary system of gestures, body deportment and facial signs to commence communication with the Eora, the newcomers seem to have taken no note of the hand and body languages which almost certainly were part of the Aboriginal 'vocabularies'. Nor were they aware of the special nuances of gesture as opposed to speech. Adam Kendon has studied sign languages in some contemporary Aboriginal communities. He has deduced that a 'user of sign language in Aboriginal society ... is regarded as communicating in an altogether different manner. To transpose one's mode of communication from the vocal medium to the kinesic medium does not only have consequences for the structure of a linguistic system. It also has consequences for how one is perceived as a social being.'

Adam Kendon, *Sign Languages of Australia: Cultural, Semiotic and Communicative Perspectives*, Melbourne: Cambridge University Press, 1988, p. 67.

1. 'When [the Aborigines] found we were not disposed to part with any more things, they entered into conversation with us, which was very fully interpreted by very plain Signs they wanted to know of what sex we were, which they explained by pointing where it was distinguishable ...'

Philip Gidley King, *The Journal of Philip Gidley King: Lieutenant, R.N. 1787-1790* (edited by Paul G. Fidlon and R. J. Ryan), Sydney: Australian Documents Library, 1980, p. 35.

WHO CONTROLS THE RUM STORE

Trade Object: Liquor decanter and goblets
Storyteller: A bourgeois woman

WOMAN: *This is a simple place for simple people. It is no great mystery how to have a good life here. Wealth can do you no harm. The secret to creating wealth in our colonies is to own the alcohol which the common people crave so much for their consolation. Rum can do us no harm at all. It is a reliable basis for our robust economy.*[1] *From there you will build empires out of other commodities.*

Take my husband. He is known far and wide as a mogul in wool.[2] *But how did we get started? As he is so fond of proclaiming, 'Who controls the brewing houses has the banks dancing a jig.'*

Research Notes

1. The officers concentrated on particular 'commodities': land, livestock, food and alcohol. By 1796 Corps officers owned 31.5% of cultivated land and 72.5% of livestock as well as a dominant influence in the trade of liquor, clothing and tobacco.

See Ross Fitzgerald and Mark Hearn, *Bligh, Macarthur and the Rum Rebellion*, Sydney: Kangaroo Press, 1988, p. 33.

2. Officers of the New South Wales Corps, most famously John Macarthur, 'used their authority to buy the cargoes of the arriving ships and sell them through middlemen to the populace. Then they moved a step further by chartering a ship, *Britannia*, to bring a mixed cargo from the Cape of Good Hope.'

David Day, *Smugglers and Sailors. The Customs History of Australia 1788-1901*, Canberra: Australian Government Publishing Services, 1992, p. 6.

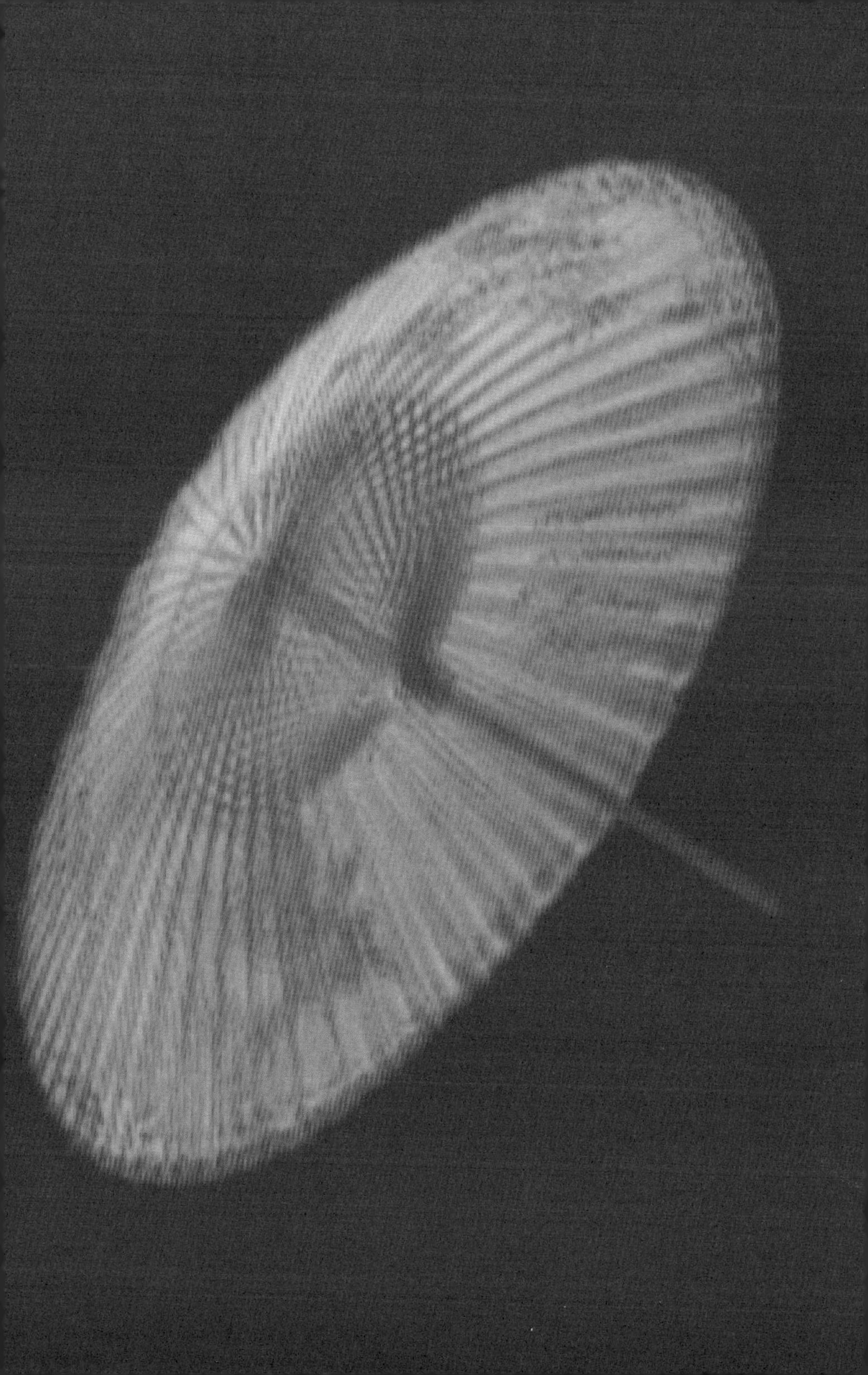

THE COAST OF NEW ZEALAND

Trade Object: Umbrellas
Storyteller: A young Irish woman in a tavern

WOMAN: *What can you rely on these days, when there's so much confusion? When there's so many decisions to be made in a day? Why, even umbrellas are a puzzle. On a nasty day in July, when you need a little shelter, how do you choose one?*

Down at Mr Campbell's store there are cane-and-paper umbrellas from Batavia. Gaudy colours such as might appeal to ruffians. There are sealskin devices made by Americans. And English instruments of black canvas and whale-bone. These are my preference. The whalebone. You remain loyal to your heart, you know. It's how you make your choices.

My sweetheart, he works on the whaleboats.[1] *He tells me that my umbrella is made with the bones from the throat of the whale. That is sufficient for me. I support my young man when I go to the store.*

He is in the south seas right now. He's looking for sandalwood now. But he tells me the whale is the thing. The whale is when he has his big time.[2] *He brings me the songs.*

[She sings 'The Coast of New Zealand', a traditional sailor's song about the South Pacific whaling grounds, adapted from 'The Banks of Newfoundland'.]*

One night as I lay in my bunk
'a dreaming all around,
I dreamt I was in a public house

back home in Sydney Town,
with my true love there aside of me
and a jug of ale in hand.
But I woke broken-hearted
off the coast of New Zealand.

Yes we'll sail around where the whales abound
till it's one last fish we'll land.
In her heart we'll strike with our deadly spikes
off the coast of New Zealand.

Oh when shall we return back home
to sleep in sheets so pure?
Well, until our ship is full of oil[3]
these chills we must endure.
But soon our days will warm with cheer
and our eyes will brim with tears,
for we'll exchange the pain for joy
with the girls we love so dear.

Yes we'll sail around where the whales abound
Till it's one last fish we'll land.
Yes we'll strike her heart with our deadly sharps,
off the coast of New Zealand.

Yes we'll bail around and we'll sail around
so far away from the banking sands.
We'll come and warm our hearts back in Sydney Town,
all away from the cold of New Zealand.

Ah yes, my adventurous young man!

*A version of this song can be heard on the recording, *Layers*, by Chris Foster, Topic Records 12TS329 (1977).

Research Notes

'Black whale oil has become very scarce, every available gallon having been shipped for the English markets.'

Sydney Gazette, June 4, 1831.

'See with what entire freedom the whaleman takes his handful of lamps – often but old bottles and vials, though – to the copper cooler at the try-works, and replenishes them there, as mugs of ale at a vat. He burns, too, the purest of oil, in its unmanufactured, and, therefore, unvitiated state; a fluid unknown to solar, lunar, or astral contrivances ashore.'

Herman Melville, *Moby-Dick*, first published in 1851, Chapter XCVII.

'In the first six months of 1802, more than 4,000 barrels of whale oil and 5,000 barrels of seal oil were brought into Sydney before being shipped off to America and Britain.'

David Day, *Smugglers and Sailors: The Customs History of Australia 1788-1901*, Canberra: Australian Government Publishing Service, 1992, p. 35.

'The *Nelson*'s sperm oil, sold last week, averaged thirty-nine pounds ten shillings per ton – cash.'

The Australian, May 4, 1832.

1. 'Many of our smartest Australian and Anglo Australian bred youth, appear to be turning themselves to sea-faring pursuits.'

The Australian, May 4, 1832.

2. '5 whalers, all fully equipped and well-manned go to sea tomorrow upon a whaling cruise. Wish them every success. "These and the wool bales – are our national sinews ...".'

The Australian, August 3, 1832.

3. 'By the 1780s the control of oil supplies had become an international issue, as the steadily expanding use of whale oil brought about a demand far exceeding the normal supply. A

spiralling consumption of oil for street lighting was developing, and even by 1780 there were more lights in London's Oxford Row than in all Paris.'

Margaret Steven, *Trade, Tactics and Territory: Britain in the Pacific 1783-1823*, Melbourne: Melbourne University Press, 1983, p. 68.

THE CURE

Trade Object: Sack of sea salt
Storyteller: An entrepreneur, now an old man

MAN: *In the old days, what was all the fuss about seals? I'll tell you. It was because of tea. We were all slaves to the drinking of tea. We had a taste for it.*[1] *And where did it come from? From China. And what did they want that we could trade with them? Nothing. They had every strange thing they needed and wanted.*

That is, until we found sandalwood for them, first thing, and until a Chinaman in Shanghai worked out how to take the fur off the skin of a seal, second thing. That was their big discovery, this second thing, and it was our big discovery too – how to make a coat and boots from the soft skin of a seal.

The way it used to be, you try to take the fur off a seal and you pull the skin apart, because it is so soft. Like making shoes out of the skin under your arm. But now the Chinamen have a way to use sealskin and so now they need something from the world. They need seals! Which goes to show ... you've always got a chance in the world.

Now we have the chance to trade skins for tea. So now I have the chance to get rich. Because I know where the seals are and there are men with ships who will trust me. Men in Sydney – Mr Lord, Mr Kable.[2] *I'm young in those days. And I know how to sail. And I don't know how to get scared yet.*

But I'm not getting rich just like that. You can kill all the seals

you like. You can tear their skins off. But it all rots like old fish. Unless you get salt for packing the skins in.

So I'm a smart man. That's true. But smart men are not always rich men, not like it's a rule you can rely on. More likely it's lucky men are rich men. And where I get lucky is Kangaroo Island. I'm catching the roaring forties back from the Cape Town, on a ship full of cattle, and the bad luck of a big storm pushes me onto this island. What do I find there? Seals, number one. Men looking like seals, number two. Runaways, ship-jumpers, blood-lovers. Some have brought black women. They are locked up on the island by the sea all around them. It's like the bible. Sodom and Gomorrah. What is the law there? This is the law there. [He shows a seal-skinning knife.] *These people are animals. That is to say, they look and smell like seals. They wear the coat of seals. They eat seals. They sleep on seals. They grunt at each other at night. Light comes from burning seals. That is to say, they live in seal skins and they set fire to a slab of dead seal. The blubber of it just burning on the ground. At night there are seals burning all over this island.*[3]

It's bad luck for me to be there? Perhaps you'd think so. Well, I was making a list, remember? Of things on the island. First: Seals. Second: men looking like seals. Third: SALT! Great rock pools of it made by the heat of the sun. Salt getting ready hundreds of years for me. The grunting men use it, in small amounts, to cure their skins. They sell bundles of skins to fools like me who pass by. But there is so much salt here.[4] *And I am no fool. For years this salt could supply industry out of Sydney. At least for years enough for me to get rich. I am talking about industry.*

The seal men have slipped back. That is to say, they can't think like me, like a man of reason, like a man of industry. I reason it

this way. I can take all their skins. I can take all the salt. There's so much salt. More than is needed for skins. I can use it in Tahiti. Because that's another thing I can be doing. I can sail a ship to Tahiti. I know winds. I know men with ships. Tahiti. Salt pork in Tahiti. Now this is perfect. I can take seal skins to China. I can swap them for tea. And then bear down on Tahiti!

On the way back from China, the ship smells like breakfast. A ship almost full with tea. But I've kept a space free down below deck. I've got three tons of salt stored in the midship, because if the winds are right and the price of pork is good in Sydney Town, I can call in at Tahiti, slaughter some swine and salt them in barrels right there in the harbour. TAHITI!

Aaaah! It was a big life in those days. To be young and without fear. To live in this town and have a ship for taking away with salt and seals that cost me nothing. Because I was there first.

It was such a life in those days!

Research Notes

'Seal oil, being clear, odourless and free from the rancid taste of whale or fish oil, could be used in foodstuffs. It burned in a bright, pure flame without smell or smoke and an ordinary wick would burn for six hours on one-sixth of a pint. The caulking of ships, the manufacture of paints and the preservation of ropes, sails and timbers, not to mention the lubrication of clocks and other new devices, depended on the supply of increasing quantities of fine animal fats.'

Margaret Steven, *Trade, Tactics and Territory: Britain in the Pacific 1783-1823*, Melbourne: Melbourne University Press, 1983, pp. 85 - 86.

'Sealing was a far-flung, expanding trade and secrecy always played a part in what was essentially an individualistic enterprise. Competitors automatically sought to conceal their intentions, routes and cargoes from one another or even from the casual enquirer.'

Margaret Steven, *Trade, Tactics and Territory: Britain in the Pacific 1783-1823*, Melbourne: Melbourne University Press, 1983, p. 100.

'Aside from his extensive agricultural interests, Macarthur also nurtured bold plans to establish Sydney as a centre of prosperous South Pacific/South-East Asia trade and had elaborate plans to use the privateer *Harrington* to open up a Sydney - Calcutta - Canton trade link in defiance of the East India Company ... Macarthur and Blaxell did use both the *Harrington* and *Parramatta* for South Pacific trading activities and in December 1807 the *Parramatta* returned to Sydney after a successful voyage to the Society Islands, laden with 75,660 pounds of pork.'

Ross Fitzgerald and Mark Hearn, *Bligh, Macarthur and the Rum Rebellion*, Sydney: Kangaroo Press, 1988, pp. 87 - 88.

See also, N. Wace and B. Lovett, *Yankee Maritime Activities and the Early History of Australia*, Canberra: ANU Press, 1973.

1. 'Europe had become dependent on Chinese import goods to an enormous degree, but especially on tea – the indispensable import ...

... ... Tea quickly became institutionalized as the national drink and the [East India] Company was required by an Act of Parliament to keep a year's supply always in stock.'

Margaret Steven, *Trade, Tactics and Territory: Britain in the Pacific 1783-1823*, Melbourne: Melbourne University Press, 1983, p. 13.

2. 'In mid-1800 Henry Kable, [a] retailing agent and James Underwood, a carpenter by trade, became partners in the sealing industry. Kable and Underwood operated their venture with ships Kable had built and launched from his yard at the mouth of the Tank Stream. It became a profitable business and Simeon Lord joined them as another partner. During the 1803 - 04 season the enterprise employed 60 men and gathered 30,000 skins from seal colonies in the Bass Strait and the Tasmanian coast.'

Ross Fitzgerald and Mark Hearn, *Bligh, Macarthur and the Rum Rebellion*, Sydney: Kangaroo Press, 1988, p. 48.

3. The Russian scientist F. G. Bellingshausen described the scene on Macquarie Island, which was supporting a rude economy identical to that of Kangaroo Island: One of the 'sealers invited us into his hut, which was about 29 feet long by 10 feet broad. Inside it was lined with skins of seals, and outside was covered with a kind of grass which grows on the island. At one end there was a small hearth, and a lamp was always kept alight. On the hearth, as wood and coal were unobtainable, there was kept burning a piece of sea elephant blubber and melted fat was used for the lamp. ... Inside it was so black and dark from the smoke that the smouldering light from the lamp and the holes in the wall, over which bladders were stretched, scarcely lit the interior of the hut, and until we got accustomed to the light the sealers had to lead us by the hand ...'

Quoted in Lyndon Rose, *Richard Siddins of Port Jackson*, Canberra: Roebuck, 1984, pp. 67 - 68.

See also E. M. Andrews, *Australia and China: The Ambiguous Relationship*, Melbourne: Melbourne University Press, 1985.

4. According to a report in the *Sydney Gazette* (April 7, 1810), Kangaroo Island was almost invariably 'overrun with formidable

gangs' of sealers and runaways. The Norfolk Island ship, *Endeavour*, survived its summer visit to the unruly location and returned to Sydney laden with '50 tons of fine bay salt' that crew members had shovelled into barrels.

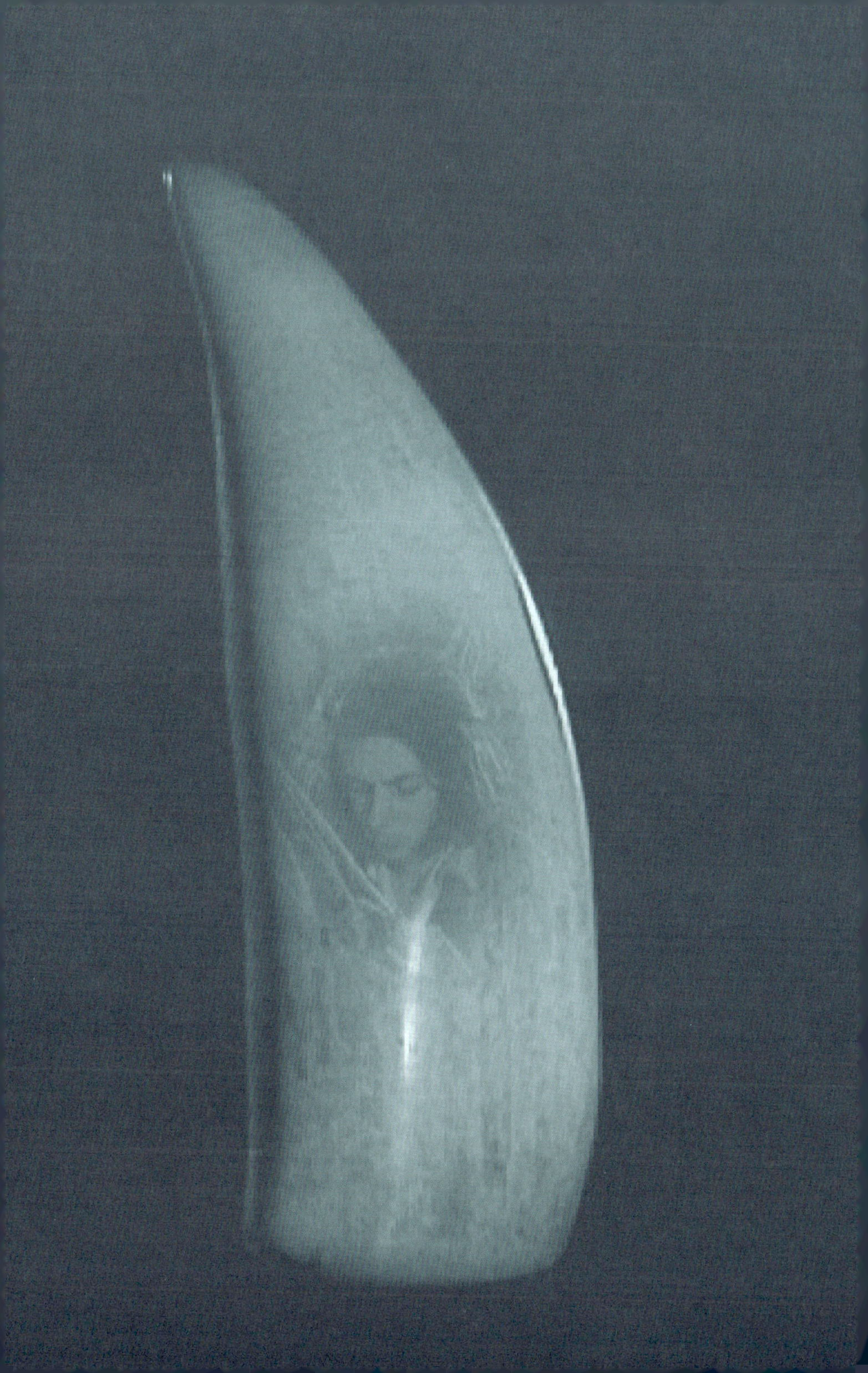

THE SECRET LANGUAGE OF TEETH

Trade Object: A whale's tooth
Storyteller: A young merchant sailor on a whaling ship

SAILOR: *Nothing gets wasted in this world. 'The devil takes whatever virtue does not claim.' And the devil makes trouble for idle hands. Nothing is wasted. That's why we take the teeth from the whale. We pop them out with a jemmy. Because we can make handles and buttons out of teeth. And we can make our hands busy too.*

When we're on the ship, we put a few teeth aside. So we can carve and talk during the night watch. To keep the devil away and the boredom too, which is the devil just waiting. Boredom is the devil inviting.

The devil can take many forms, I say.[1] *The last tour we took – three years in Pacific waters – the devil was the Captain. He had hate in his eye. Hate for something that happened long ago. And here we were in front of him, so we were the ones he could hurt for the thing that hurt him, whatever it was, all that time ago.*

This is the cruellest thing: he did not let us talk or sing when we were on watch. How can a man know his own mind if he can't speak it out loud and build his mind's shapes with other minds speaking the same way?[2] *The Captain, he says that there is work to be done and that talking is a dodge against work. He says we are on a factory out here in the sea and therefore we will behave like wretches in any factory. If we were not wretches we would be a Captain like him.*[3]

He was thinking he could stop us making ourselves as people with minds and opinions. He was thinking he could make us into nothing, nothing but muscle for making another man's money. Thinking we would surrender our minds to the rule of his quiet. Not speaking out loud on the decks.

But sailors use a secret language for remembering, so we can talk the important things, the first chance we get. We've found a secret way to put our thoughts in store so we can bring them out later and build our minds with them each chance we get to talk out loud in the open, away from the factory. This makes us smile sly. The devil is in his cabin writing down words on a page, thinking he is the only one writing sensible things.

What am I talking about? The secret language of teeth! We put some whales teeth aside and we scratch on them during the watch.[4] *We're making no noise. We're not doing any talking. We're not writing down words. That's what it looks like. The devil-Captain looks at us. What does he see? Just fools scratching like dogs on a bone. He thinks he's put his fear of the devil in us. But we have kept ourselves busy to ward off this devil. What he doesn't know is we've been talking to each other all the time in the scratching. But it's not till we get downstairs that we make it all come out loud, with some ink or some soot from the smoke of burning fat. We are not so quiet as he thinks.*

[The sailor takes some oil and soot from the glass of the lamp behind him. As he wipes this grime across the whale tooth he has been scratching, the oil makes a scene emerge, an allegorical tableau showing the Captain as a devil overlooking crew members who are working like bullocks hauling a dray with sails.]

Research Notes

'"Nor could I think what world I was in," one boy remembered of his first going to sea, "whether among spirits or devils. All seemed strange; different language and strange expression of tongue, that I thought myself always asleep or in a dream, and never properly awake." Many things in this peculiar life were always quite different from life ashore, but most things afloat themselves varied depending on whether the ship were at sea or in port. To weigh or drop anchor made a revolution in the internal affairs of every ship, suddenly altering the rhythms of daily life.'

N.A.M. Rodger, *The Wooden World: An Anatomy of the Georgian Navy*, Annapolis, Maryland: Naval Institute Press, 1986, p. 37.

'When first they impressed me and sent me to sea,
'Twas in the winter time in the making of the hay,
They sent me on board of a shipped called *Torbay*,
Oh! her white muzzle guns they did sore frighten me.

Says the boatswain to Paddy, And what has brought you here?
For the making of hay 'tis the wrong time of year.
By Jasus, says Paddy, I wish I was gone,
For your small wooden kingdom I don't understand.

Oh! the first thing they gave me it was a long sack,
Which they told me to get in and lay on my back;
I lay on my back till the clock struck one bell,
And the man overhead he sung out, All is well.'

James Anthony Gardner, *Above and Under Hatches: being Naval Recollections in shreds and patches with strange reflections, written in 1836*, edited by Christopher Lloyd, London: Batchworth, 1955, p. 63.

'English society in the middle years of the [eighteenth] century was, or at least seemed to be, fundamentally secure and almost static. Those in positions of power or authority, and those without either, felt themselves far more bound by mutual ties of dependence and obligation than separated by divisions of class. Forty years later, at the time of the great naval mutinies of 1797 [after the great political revolutions of Europe], officers and ratings spoke and acted as though they perceived class interests at work which united lower deck and quarter deck against each other.'

N.A.M. Rodger, *The Wooden World: An Anatomy of the Georgian Navy*, Annapolis, Maryland: Naval Institute Press, 1986, p. 206.

1. In *Mr Bligh's Bad Language*, Greg Dening ponders the dramas on the mutinous *Bounty* in order to understand the power of discipline, persuasion and allegiance in late eighteenth-century English culture: 'If we would understand [the *Bounty*], we must catch in it some of the tension that Europe was experiencing as it changed its systems of social control. We must catch it up in the question of what it took to control an institution of discipline, like the navy, when those subject to that discipline were being relativised by new political experiences around them and new cultural experiences of otherness. It took management, not violence.'

Greg Dening, *Mr Bligh's Bad Language: Passion, Power, and Theatre on the* Bounty, Cambridge: Cambridge University Press, 1992, p. 123.

2. 'the seamen and landmen, servants and petty officers of each part of the ship were divided into two parties, the starboard and larboard watches, and ... not less than one whole watch was on deck at all times, night and day. Each watch lasted four hours, except for the two two-hour dog watches between four and eight in the evening, which made the number of watches in the day an odd number and so ensured that the duties of each watch continually varied. The changing of the watch marked the passage of time aboard ship, where no clock would run. A petty officer ... kept a half-hour sand-glass; when it turned, he rang the ship's bell, and at eight bells the watch changed.'

N.A.M. Rodger, *The Wooden World: An Anatomy of the Georgian Navy*, Annapolis, Maryland: Naval Institute Press, 1986, p. 39.

3. 'The working and living conditions of the eighteenth-century sailor were as confined, dangerous and noisome as the factory or prison. The stench, the grime and the dark ... Fourteen inches' breadth was the permitted space for a man to sling his hammock. When Roderick Random was shown his berth, he was "filled with astonishment and horror. We descended by divers ladders to a space as dark as a dungeon." Doctor Johnson was adamant in his view that their situation was worse than prison: "No man will be a sailor who has a contrivance to get himself into a gaol; for being in a ship is being in gaol with the chance of being drowned." Shipboard discipline was, if anything, worse than factory discipline.'

Peter Linebaugh, *The London Hanged: Crime and Civil Society in the Eighteenth Century*, Harmondsworth: Penguin, 1991, p. 130.

4. 'Throughout the Pacific, and also in Nantucket, and New Bedford, and Sag Harbour, you will come across lively sketches of whales and whaling-scenes, graven by the fishermen themselves on Sperm Whale-teeth, or ladies' busks wrought out of the Right Whale-bone, and other like skrim-shander articles, as the whalemen call the numerous little ingenious contrivances they elaborately carve out of the rough material, in their hours of ocean leisure. Some of them have little boxes of dentistical-looking implements, specially intended for the skrimshandering business. But, in general, they toil with their jack-knives alone; and, with that almost omnipotent tool of the sailor, they will turn you out anything you please, in the way of a mariner's fancy.'

Herman Melville, *Moby-Dick*, first published 1851, Chapter LVII.

THE TOUCH OF GENTLENESS BROUGHT AT LAST TO THE COLONY

Trade Object: Sewing kit and pin-cushion
Storyteller: An ex-convict seamstress

SEAMSTRESS: *What did I do during the war? I fought for my life is what I did. This 'war' I'd be speaking about, it's me and the girls all arriving on the whale boats. The 'Third Fleet', they're calling it these days. The ships smelt like dead fish in every plank of wood. We were being carried like mouthfuls of food down in the belly of a whale. That's what they were using, whale boats to move us.*

At Port Jackson, they unloaded us like cargo and then went off on their real work. Chasing the whale, like boys out on the skylark. And here we were, hundreds of lady Jonahs spilled out on the harbour for another pack of men, these ones acting like sharks. Like they've been hungry for ages.

That day we arrived, my god, who could forget it? Women, brought into the prisons and into the army camps. What were we for? Well, I'll tell you. We were for turning a gaol into 'society'. Like as if a woman is magic.

Sure, if I could tell you the day we arrived! It was men consuming us like we were morsels for the belly of a beast. And nobody told us, I mean to say, nobody had warned us. But it was the use they were making of us. We were 'the first touch of gentleness brought at last to the colony'. I heard an officer say that!

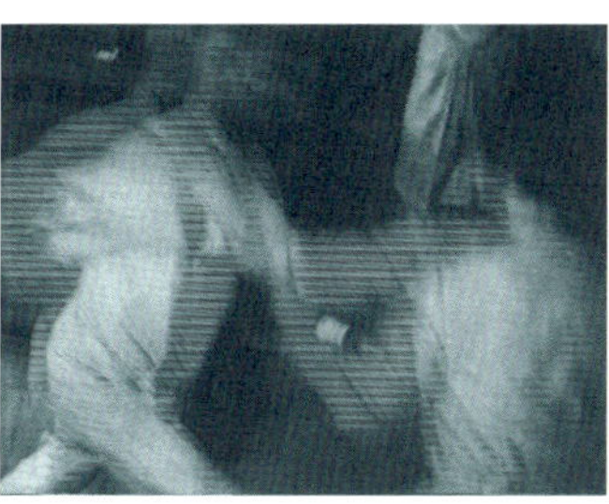

Research Notes

After completing its duties as a First Fleet transport ship, 'the *Lady Penryhn* sailed from Botany Bay on 5 May 1788 for China by way of Tahiti and arrived at Macao on 19 October. The *Prince of Wales* returned to England. The voyages of these two vessels gave the whalemen an opportunity to learn something of the seas whose potential was virtually unknown. Champion and Curtis discovered whales near Madagascar and saw numbers of whales in the Indian Ocean. Their discoveries off the coast of New Holland or Van Diemen's Land received little publicity. Nevertheless the Third Fleet of ten transport vessels and H.M.S. *Gorgon* that left England for Port Jackson early in 1791 included five more southern whaling vessels.'

Margaret Steven, *Trade, Tactics and Territory: Britain in the Pacific 1783-1823*, Melbourne: Melbourne University Press, p. 80.

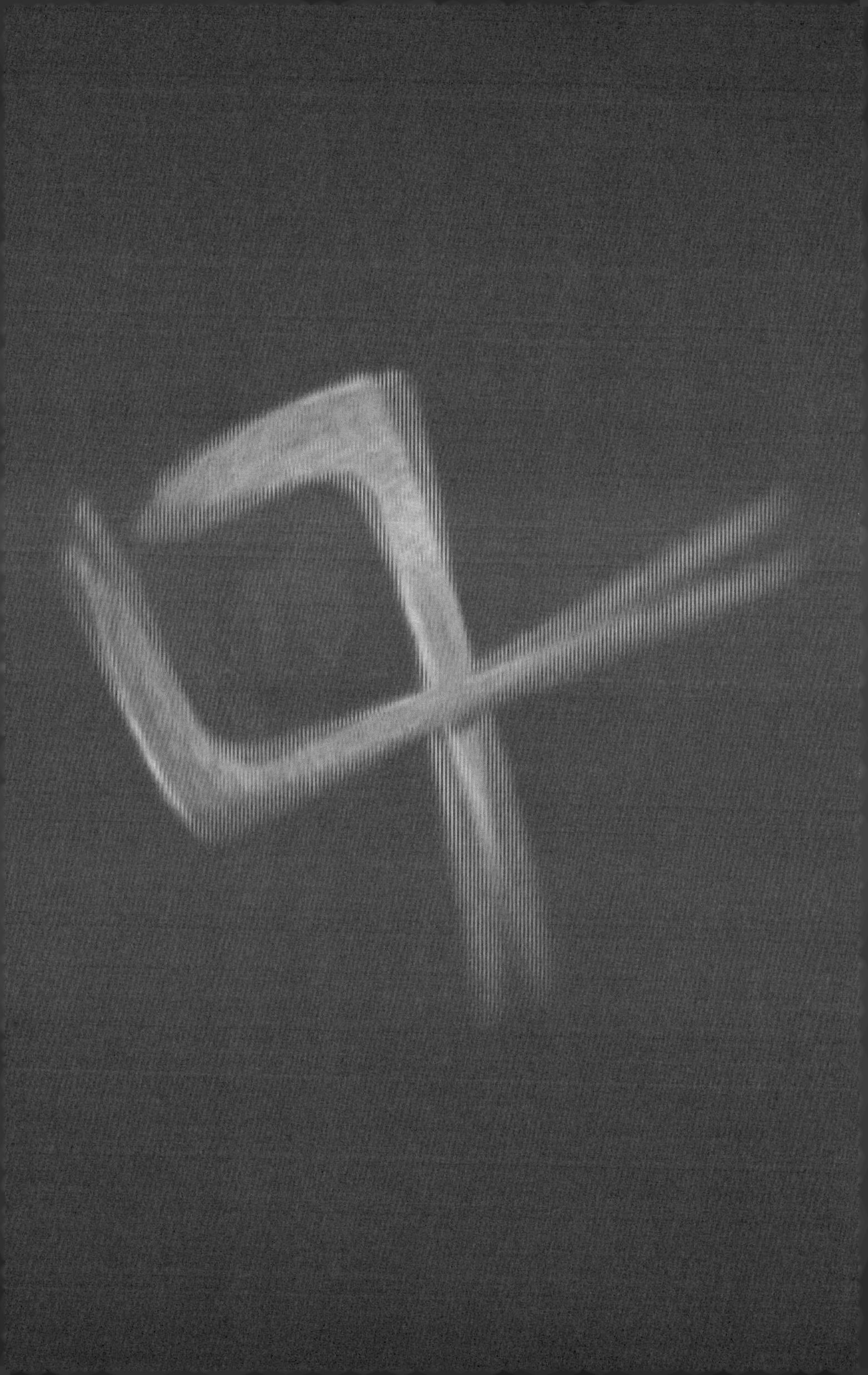

TWO DISTANT PLANETS

Trade Objects: Aboriginal throwing sticks
Storyteller: Russian scientist

SCIENTIST: *In year eighteen hundred and twenty, I was guest of Governor Macquarie, when my ship was in Sydney Town. So much was to learn in those days. The natives of Parramatta were still present in numbers and Mr Macquarie gave us leave to investigate wherever we wanted.*[1]

It is the natives that intrigue me. But who understands these people? On some nights I would walk into their camp and receive gestures of welcome. There were objects for barter. To take back to Russia. With rum could you buy most things in those times. But on other nights, I was made to feel like an intruder. Once I came upon a ceremony of dance. They were entirely discourteous.

So, in some degree of anger, I walked away, up to the cliff that loomed over our tents. This is where I stood and beheld. I looked now at the distant lights of Sydney Town, now at the woods where I had lately seen the darkness of half-naked demons and their wild amusements. The same moon shone down on both places; the same foliage, the same flowers beautified the earth, there and here ... Yet it seemed to me that the mouth of the little Parramatta River separated two quite distant planets.[2]

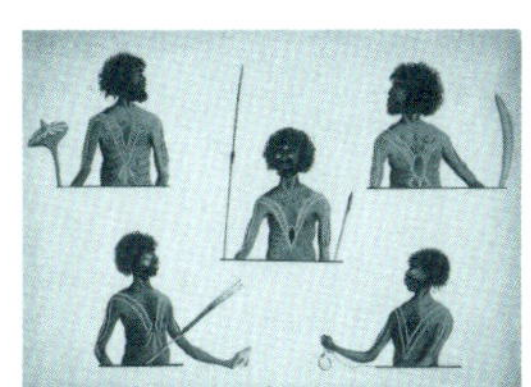

Research Notes

Most Europeans felt self-righteous about seizing and exploiting Aboriginal property. But even the most self-assured newcomers admitted that their understanding of indigenous customs and beliefs was extremely rudimentary. Watkin Tench, for example, confessed his confusions on April 13, 1791: 'To comprehend the reasons which induce an Indian to perform many of the offices of life is difficult: to pronounce that which could encourage hope, or stimulate industry, to attempt its penetration.'

Watkin Tench, *Sydney's First Four Years*, Sydney: Library of Australian History, 1979, p. 228.

Many of the colonists were poignantly aware of how equally estranged each culture – incumbent and incursive – was to the other. Matthew Flinders, for example, described an encounter at Twofold Bay in 1798: 'Our attention was suddenly called by the screams of three women, who took up their children and ran off in great consternation. Soon afterwards a man made his appearance. He was of middle age, unarmed except with a whaddie or wooden scimitar, and came up to us seemingly with careless confidence. We made much of him, and gave him some biscuit; and he in return presented us with a piece of fat, probably a whale. This I tasted; but, watching an opportunity to spit out when he should not be looking; I perceived him doing precisely the same thing with our biscuit, whose taste was probably no more agreeable to him than his whale was to me. ... The commencement of our trigonometrical operations was seen by him with indifference, if not contempt; and he quitted us, apparently satisfied that, from people who could thus occupy themselves seriously, there was nothing to be apprehended.'

Flinders' H.M.S. *Norfolk* journal, quoted in Max Colwell, *The Voyages of Matthew Flinders*, Sydney: Paul Hamlyn, 1970, p. 43.

Scientists occasionally described encounters in which the Aborigines seemed to be making quite pointed interpretations and dismissals of scientific procedure. In August 1814, for example, the Russian astronomer A. Rossysky related a telling scene:

'Mr de Silvier and I went to check the chronometers on Benelong's Point, and there we met with a curious incident. We had only made a few preliminary readings when we caught sight of five natives, including a woman. They were approaching us. Having our astronomical instruments with us, we were rather nervous lest the natives disturb them; but then we calmed down, thinking that the natives had not spotted us. To the contrary, they came straight to us and sat close by on the grass, repeating many words that they had learned from the English: 'How do you do?' and 'Very well'. They looked at the sextant, chronometer, and artificial horizon with astonishment ... Whilst I had been pouring out the mercury, and Mr de Silvier removing our sextant from them, one native had discovered the chronometer and was showing its moving second hand to his fellows, in amazement. All then drew close to the instrument and, no matter how hard I tried to keep them off, they stubbornly insisted that I show it to them – to such a point, indeed, that they began seriously to alarm me by indicating their weapons. So, to satisfy them, I was forced to take off my own watch, which also had a second hand, and to show them its inside. Their wonder at the sight of the pendulum, which shone in their eyes, was indescribable. They handed the watch around delightedly, and I failed to observe how ultimately one of their number took up a twig and thrust it between the wheels, which made the watch stop. This so irritated me that I took the watch back and started to drive them away; but Mr de Silvier advised me to be more circumspect since they were five and we – only two. After remaining a few minutes longer, the natives laughed loudly and went off.'

Rossysky was keen to interpret childlike wonder in the Aborigines' response to the gadgets of science. Hence he 'failed to observe' that he had just been made the butt of a canny ensemble joke.

See Glynn Barratt, *The Russians at Port Jackson 1814–1822*, Canberra: Australian Institute of Aboriginal Studies, 1981, pp. 24 - 25.

The looting of artefacts quickly contributed to the souring of relations between Aborigines and Europeans. On November 16, 1788, Governor Arthur Phillip wrote to English Government Secretary Stephens:

'The natives now avoid us more than they did when we first landed, and which I impute to the robberies committed on them by the convicts, who steal their spears and fizgigs, which they frequently leave in their huts when they go out a-fishing, and which the people belonging to the transports purchase, though every possible precaution has been taken to prevent it.'

Arthur Phillip, 'Governor Phillip to Secretary Stephens' in *Historical Records of Australia*, 1788, p. 100.

See also, Greg Dening, 'Southern Cross/Northern Crosses: The Poetics of Hemisphere', in John Hardy and Alan Frost (eds) *Studies from Terra Australis to Australia*, Canberra: Australian Academy of the Humanities, 1988.

1. Between the years 1807 and 1825, ten Russian expeditions of science and survey put in at Sydney. Out of these interactions, a huge haul of contact-period Eora artefacts was taken to Russia, where they are still sequestered.

Ivan Mikhaylovich Simonov visited Sydney in 1820, as ethnologist and physicist aboard the ship *Vostok*. Much of his time was spent observing and 'negotiating' with the Aborigines in and around Sydney Town. He was a conscientious diarist: 'The natural conditions in New Holland likewise exercised an influence over the tribes of men who had arrived in times immemorial. Broadly speaking those tribes are as wild and unlovely as the inhabited Australian continent. The English have settled in the best parts of the country.'

Glynn Barratt, *The Russians at Port Jackson 1814–1822*, Canberra: Australian Institute of Aboriginal Studies, 1981, p. 49.

2. The Captain of the *Vostok* was Fabian Gottlieb Bellingshausen. He was a keen chronicler of the interactions between the Aborigines and the Europeans: 'Because the natives are so accustomed to the nomadic life, it has not proved possible to induce them to settle in any one place. In spite of all Governor Macquarie's efforts, few

natives have attached themselves to the colony. The elders of the native groups are distinguished by copper signs with an inscription giving their name and the place where they mostly reside; these they wear by a copper chain at their chest. The elders are sometimes useful to the government in cases of pursuit of, or searches for, escaped convicts. The government gives them boats for fishing and to facilitate their movements across water.'

Glynn Barratt, *The Russians at Port Jackson 1814–1822*, Canberra: Australian Institute of Aboriginal Studies, 1981, p. 38.

Bellingshausen considered himself free to mingle with the Aboriginal communities. 'At night, out of curiosity, we once went to see what night arrangements our friends had, and how they slept. At our approach, their faithful dog started to bark and they at once awoke. Seeing us, Boongaree stood up and came up to us, but the others remained in the positions where they had been lying. A few fires smouldered between them as they peacefully slept, the men together with the women. Fires warmed them on both sides.'

Glynn Barratt, *The Russians at Port Jackson 1814–1822*, Canberra: Australian Institute of Aboriginal Studies, 1981, p. 36.

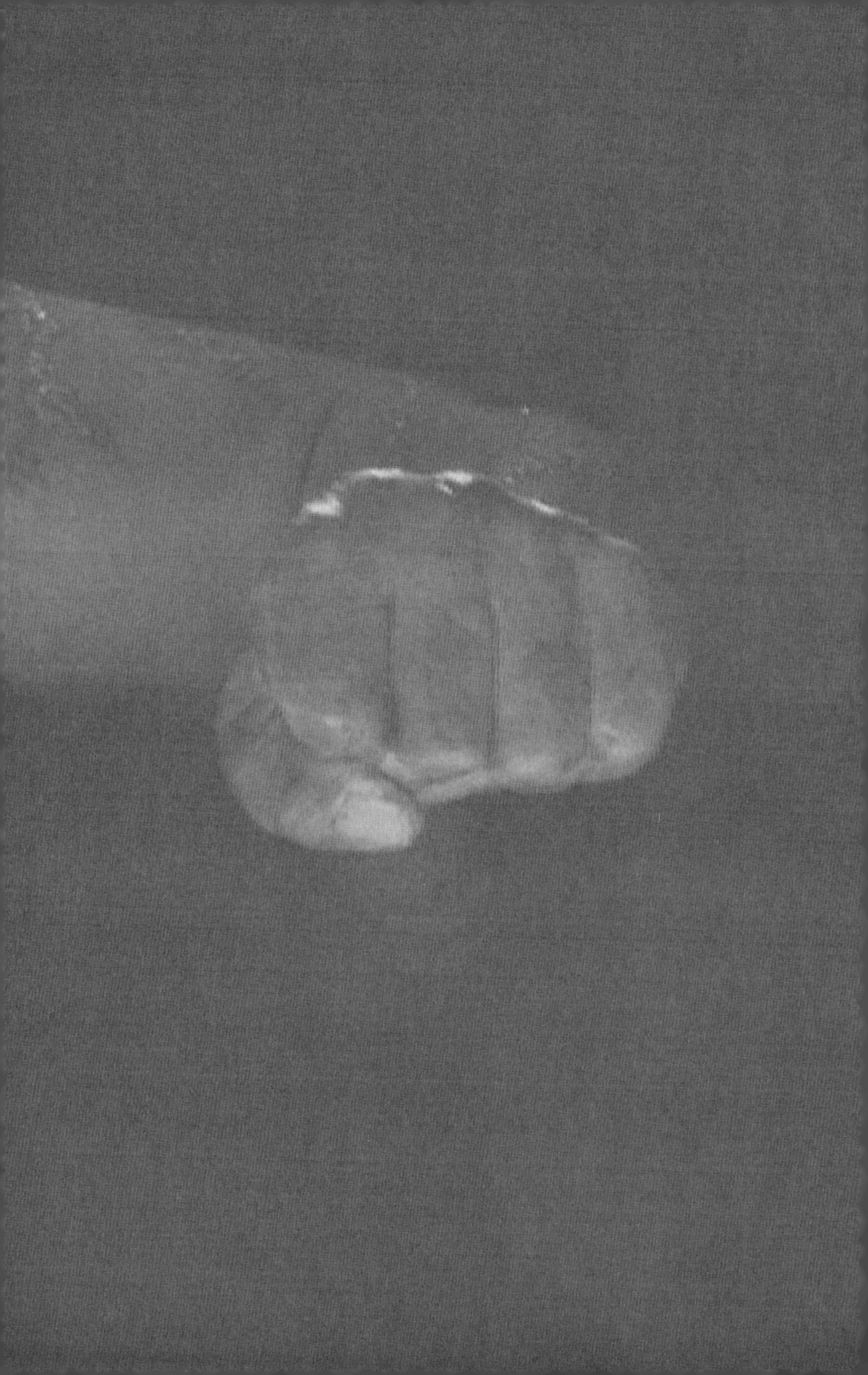

WALKING OUR STREETS THIS MORNING

Trade Object: Walking stick of wood and whalebone
Storyteller: A heavily scarred Islander man

MAN: *We were on our way home with only half a load of wood. Sydney ships have been coming for thirty years, and there is no sandalwood left on most of the islands. I am certain of this. But the Captain is angry. 'The islanders are holding on to the wood.' So says the Captain. What will we do? Go back to Sydney Town[1] with the hold half full of air? No, we tack against the wind, till we raise the Isle of Pines. We row the launch over coral and call to the pine men. But it's the same declaration. 'No wood remaining,' say the men who come down to the beach. 'No wood remaining here on our island.'*

Have you ever seen an angry man turn into a mad man? Have you ever seen one crazy man become twenty like him? The Captain takes a cutlass and chops at the black man who said no. In the row boat, we are blinking. One of us is sick into the water. A noise like a seal. Suddenly we are all angry men who are frightened men also. I am standing in the boat, because I am one of the crew. But these are not my people. Time was when I am a Fiji man.[2] But I am Sydney man now. Time was when I am a whale man. It's how I came to Sydney Town.[3] As a whale man. But now I am a wood man. Can wood do you harm? I did not think so.

The frightened men pull on the oars. Too quick they pull. This one boat is too much like twenty tuna-fish going every way. The boat jumps like twenty fish. I fall in the water. Now I am two

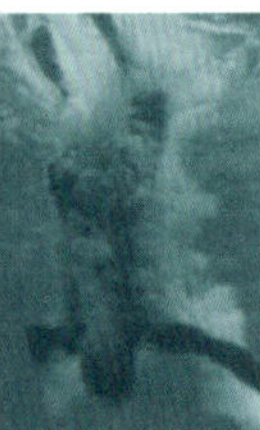

things. I am a black man in the water and I am a man from the boat. Island men have knives. White men have knives. White men hack me. Black men stab me. The water is red. It is angry and frightened. Who is not frightened? There are men and pieces of men in the water. Did I say I was two things? In the water I am thinking, 'soon I will be many things ... many pieces of me and then I will be dead.'

Black men are red in the water. Now white man are dead there too.

A white man takes me by the hair and pulls me to the boat. Another white man hits this man with a knife. They are all angry men, but the First Mate still has me by the hair and he knows it is me. He calls out my name and the boat men look at me like I am all at once turning white there in front of them.

They row angry away from red water. Cannonballs bounce across the water. Our ship is sending out cannonballs! I look back at the beach and I see black men spin in the air. Pieces of them come off like a dog shakes away water.

The rowboat moves like one thing now, because the oars are going together. I call out the stroke, which is always my job. 'Stroke.' 'Stroke.' 'Stroke.' It is like I am watching me do this. Watching me looking at the beach and looking at the ship.

We climb on the ship and we come back to Sydney and nobody is happy. Because we only got half a load of wood. But we are back in the city. We wash and shave and put on shoes and white shirts. Any morning, you might see one of us walking down Pitt Street. Like as if we are peaceable and contented.

Research Notes

'Islanders – first Polynesians, later Melanesians – were employed in large numbers aboard the ships of European whalers and traders which entered the Pacific from the end of the eighteenth century. Most were paid less than equivalent white sailors, but many, nevertheless, sought work in the shipping trade where they quickly gained a reputation as skilled and daring sailors. Because they were cheap to employ, cheap to maintain, locally available, and could be employed seasonally, especially in whaling, they reduced the costs to shipowners.'

Marion Diamond, 'Queequeg's Crewmates: Pacific Islanders in the European Shipping Industry', in *International Journal of Maritime History*, Vol. I, No. 2 (1989), p. 126.

'We would direct particular attention to the case of a vessel which sailed from Sydney two or three weeks ago, we believe, on a second voyage to the South Sea Islands. This vessel, having been chartered by a house in Sydney, left for her former voyage on the 26th of July, 1842, and arrived at the Isle of Pines on the 3rd of August. During her cruise among the sandal wood islands, there is good reason to believe the conduct of those in command of her was open to the gravest charges. We confine ourselves to this vessel as an example of these southern rovers, because she furnishes the best authenticated case within our knowledge, of their lawless conduct ... At one of the first islands where this vessel touched, a native, who had stolen a spoon from the cook, was seized, hoisted up to the rigging by the handcuffs previously fastened round his wrists, and flogged till the blood started from his body. There were two sets of men on board; the charterers had engaged a company in Sydney, and there was the original crew of the vessel. The former were probably old hands among the islands; the latter were all new to such scenes, and were at first backward in the work they were required to engage in. But it is curious to note how soon men are tutored into evil-doing, even though blood forms part of the ceremony of initiation

... At another time, at the same place, one of the ship's guns, heavily loaded with missiles, was levelled at a crowd of sixty or seventy natives standing on the beach; and only for the interposition of Providence, (for it cannot be ascribed to mere chance) in the gun's missing fire, the mind is horrified to think of the slaughter which might have been the consequence ... The natives were standing on the beach, on their own soil; and the only pretence for firing upon them was that "the bl—y natives should be punished for not bringing more wood".'

Sydney Weekly Register, May 4, 1844.

See also, Wade Doak, *The Burning of the Boyd: A Saga of Culture Clash*, Auckland: Hodder and Stoughton, 1984.

1. 'It was in the final phase of the Pacific Islands sandalwood trade that Australian merchants predominated. In the first three sandalwood rushes in the Pacific Islands they had been outstripped by English traders ... and by the bold captains from the east coast of America.'

Dorothy Shineberg, *They Came for Sandalwood. A Study of the Sandalwood Trade in the South-West Pacific 1830-1865*, Melbourne: Melbourne University Press, 1967, p. 9.

2. 'By the early nineteenth century emancipist businessmen in New South Wales had interests in land, manufacturing and shipbuilding. They were among the first to send ships to the Pacific Islands such as Fiji to obtain sandalwood ... Lord's ship, the *Marcia*, returned from Fiji with the first cargo of sandalwood in 1805.'

Ross Fitzgerald and Mark Hearn, *Bligh, Macarthur and the Rum Rebellion*, Sydney: Kangaroo Press, 1988, pp. 48 - 49.

3. In 1805, Governor King noted how Sydney thronged with 'Otaheitans, Sandwich Islanders and New Zealanders'.

Historical Records of New Zealand, Vol. I, No. 2, pp. 257 - 258.

WEALTH IS WHAT YOU SET YOUR MIND TO

Trade Object: Earthenware jar with dried beans
Storyteller: A middle-aged woman shop-keeper

WOMAN: *I was here when the Second Fleet came in. Well, to be sure, you have the genius in you ... This means I was in the First Fleet. And I was married to no military man. So have you figured me out yet? ... Can I go on? ... I was here when the Second Fleet came in. Yes, we were starving.*[1] *Yes, we were mad, almost, with lonesomeness. Yes, the new faces, yes the letters ... 'News burst upon us like meridian splendor on a blind man'. That's Mr Tench talking. An officer. 'News burst upon us like meridian splendor on a blind man'. He wrote it all down. What it was like. And I'm not here to argue with Mr Tench.*

All I will say is I saw one or two things, that day. Things that were obvious to me. While everyone else was full of other concerns. Yes. Yes. Three hundred dead had been thrown overboard.[2] *Yes, yes. Five hundred were sick when they unloaded them here. Yes. Yes. More than one hundred died within days of arrival. 'GREAT LAMENTATION!' 'TERRIBLE SHAME!' 'THE PRISONERS HAD BEEN STARVED ALMOST UNTO DEATH!' Yes. Yes. Yes.*

Do you know what I noticed? How the Captains opened up their stores and sold everything which they had kept from the prisoners. They had stored up so much food and drink. Is this a great scandal? Well I suppose it is. But do you know how much

money they made in a day? And do you think anyone with a tiny piece of finance refrained from their purchases? Don't make me laugh!

So, here is a market with an appetite unlike any other. What don't these people have? You work it out. (You don't even need to have the genius in you.) You work it out and you bring it to them. AND YOU GET TO BE RICH. That's what I saw on that day. People dead and dying. Well, my heart bleeds. But life goes on. And what is left for the living? Why, there is wealth, for one thing. And what is wealth? Wealth is what you set your mind to. Wealth is what all the other people want. And trade is what makes wealth.

So, here we are, in this place where even the prisoners are units of wealth. Truly this is a new world to rejoice in!

Research Notes

1. 'June 1790 ... I was sitting in my hut, musing on our fate, when a confused clamour in the street drew my attention. I opened my door, and saw several women with children in their arms running to and fro with distracted looks, congratulating each other, and kissing their infants with the most passionate and extravagant marks of fondness. I needed no more; but instantly started out, and ran to a hill, where, by the assistance of a pocket-glass, my hopes were realized. My next-door neighbour, a brother-officer, was with me; but we could not speak; we wrung each other by the hand, with eyes and hearts overflowing. Finding that the governor intended to go immediately in his boat down the harbour, I begged to be of his party ... The weather was wet and tempestuous; but the body is delicate only when the soul is at ease. We pushed through wind and rain, the anxiety of our sensations every moment redoubling. At last we read the word London on her stern. "Pull away, my lads! she is from Old England! a few strokes more, and we shall be aboard! hurrah for a belly-full, and news from our friends!"'

Watkin Tench, *Sydney's First Four Years, Sydney: Library of Australian History*, 1979, p. 169.

2. 'Two hundred and seventy-three convicts had their hollow corpses committed to the deep while en route from England. Of the four hundred and eighty-six convicts landed sick in Sydney, one hundred and twenty-four would not long survive their arrival ... But [with the Second Fleet in the harbour] trade had arrived in Sydney.'

David Day, *Smugglers and Sailors. The Customs History of Australia 1788–1901*, Canberra: Australian Government Publishing Services, 1992, p. 3.

'We learned that they had been almost eleven months on their passage, having left Plymouth, into which port they had put in July, 1789. We continued to ask a thousand questions on a breath. Stimulated by curiosity, they inquired in turn; but the right of being first answered, we thought, lay on our side. "Letters!

Letters!" was the cry. They were produced, and torn open in trembling agitation. News burst upon us like meridian splendor on a blind man. We were overwhelmed with it; public, private, general, and particular. Nor was it until some days had elapsed, that we were able to methodize it, or reduce it into form. We now heard for the first time of our sovereign's illness, and his happy restoration to health. The French revolution of 1789, with all the attendant circumstances of that wonderful and unexpected event, succeeded to amaze us.'

Watkin Tench, *Sydney's First Four Years, Sydney: Library of Australian History*, 1979, p. 170.

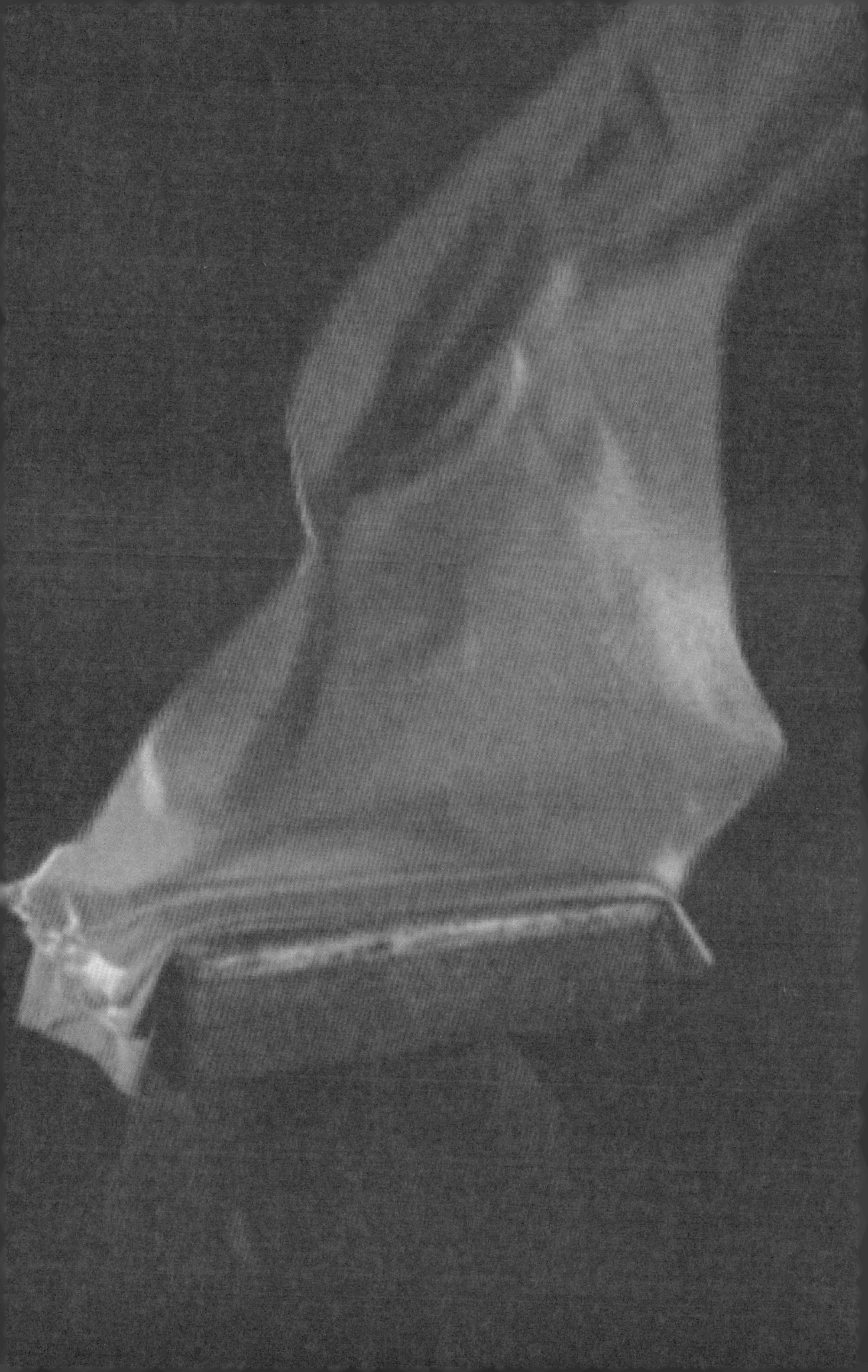

WHAT IS SO VEXATIOUS ABOUT THIS COLOUR RED?

Trade Object: A bolt of red cloth
Storyteller: An officer in the Marines

OFFICER: *In the third year at Botany Bay I was involved in a dispute.*[1] *A length of red cloth came in on a ship by way of the African Cape. But there was no label on it. No way to prove who had dispatched it.*

This same craft has letters. My mother writing to tell of a gift. She says she's sending the makings of a fine coat. This was my cloth.

My rival is also an officer. He has orders with the merchants in the Cape Town.[2] *He has receipts and dockets ... in this town full of forgers he utters such documents!*

What is there to do? He is no man to admire. But he has connived with the forgers. Let him have the cloth! Let me make the sacrifice! Let me be the white man. For the sake of peace, I withdraw from contention.

What is it about the colour red that brings us down to such passion? The black men steal our red signal flags. They tear down the king's ensign and cut away the red stripes. In Tahiti, also, the brown men have done this. A bird with red feathers must live in fear of its life.

Yes. Yes. I know what you'll tell me: 'No matter what colour the skin, we all of us bleed red so long as we're alive.' But I was sure we were above all this, us officers of the king. Us white men. I was sure we were not such slaves to our passions.

I hate the man who's wearing my coat.

Research Notes

'Sydney
August 7th. 1791

Dr. Clark

On my arrival at this place from Norfolk Island I found a piece of Scarlet Cloath in the Qr. Masters Store which I have every Reason to suppose belongs to me but as I have understood that you had Great Quantity of things coming out to you from England I would not take it untill I know if you had any Claim to it although I believe Every officer here has allowed it to be mine.

... I Remain
Dr. Clark Yours
Geo: Johnston'

Paul G. Fidlon and R. J. Ryan (eds), *The Journal and Letters of Lt. Ralph Clark 1787-1792*, Sydney: Australian Documents Library, 1981, pp. 295 - 96.

1. 'I wish to be away from this place for the place begins to be disagreeable for a great manny of my Brother officers if not all are jealous of me because I am greatly in favour with Majr. Ross – if it is so the[y] have no Occation for if I could I would not doe them an injury although manny of them would me ...'

Paul G. Fidlon and R. J. Ryan (eds), *The Journal and Letters of Lt. Ralph Clark 1787-1792*, Sydney: Australian Documents Library, 1981, p. 163.

2. 'Creswell I doe not like because he don't wish me well ... I am Certain that he would doe me all injury in his power but I am awair of him from information that has been given me that he will if he can – therfor I will take care of him – I don't care how much he grins but by God he must not attemp to bite for if he dose this world will be to Small for both of use to live in and that I believe he knows or he would have Shown his Teeth more than he has done.'

Paul G. Fidlon and R. J. Ryan (eds), *The Journal and Letters of Lt. Ralph Clark 1787-1792*, Sydney: Australian Documents Library, 1981, p. 190.

WHO CAN SING WITH ME NOW?

Trade Object: A horse in a stable
Storyteller: Young African woman

WOMAN: *In Mauritius I worked in the cane fields. A white man on a horse looked down on us all day. He told me the horse came from Australia.*[1] *He was talking sweet to me that day. You know what he was after.*

We worked together, you know. A gang of us. My mother and me. In rhythm, in the sun. We sang songs my mother remembered from the village in Mozambique. From before they stole her and put her on the island. I was born in Mauritius. I was born in slavery. I don't know my father.

When we cut the white man's cane into bundles, we sang corn planting songs from the village in Africa. But we changed them and called them sugar songs.

[She sings a verse of a Mozambique worksong.]

Oui, oui, mes enfants
il faut travailler
pour avoir son pain.

Yes, yes, my children,
you'll work this hard
if you want your bread.

When the British came to Mauritius, I hoped to go free. But there was no change. Do you know how hard it is to keep going, once you have been disappointed? I felt the hunger much harder then. I had no hope any more. I could not find it in my heart to sing any more. I stole food from the horses. I acted with no caution. I cared about nothing.

What is mad in the mind of the world? What do you think they do with me? They take me to Australia.[2] *The place with the horses. The place with the prisoners. Now they call me 'prisoner'. Why bother change the name for whatever I am? It still means I have no freedom.*

There are black people in Australia! I don't talk their language. But my new masters here, they worry that we will 'associate', the black people and me. Prisoners work in the wheat fields. At Parramatta. This is what I know how to do, from my days in Mauritius, to work in the fields. But there are black people at Parramatta. So they will not send me there. Because I might 'associate' with them. What do they think can happen?

But this is my good luck. I work with the horses. I clean their houses and wash their brown skins. But the sugar songs are no good for this work. I am learning new songs. From the Welsh boy who works with me. I learn songs from his village.

What is mad in the mind of the world?

[She sings a verse of a traditional Welsh song.]

Look, my love, the stars are shining,
all through the night,
guiding, guarding and beguiling,
all through the night.

Though old age brings grief and sorrow,
from each other we can borrow
faith in our sublime tomorrow,
all through the night.

Research Notes

'In the 1780s four Afro-American Londoners were among the first convicts transported to Botany Bay.'

Peter Linebaugh, *The London Hanged: Crime and Civil Society in the Eighteenth Century*, Harmondsworth: Penguin, 1991, p. 414.

1. 'The *Dart* made regular voyages to Australia [from Mauritius] with cargoes of sugar [in return for cattle, horses, timber and coal from New South Wales] and in 1834 she carried a Mauritian slave named Azor. He was sentenced to permanent transportation to New South Wales for theft. Also on board were two young Mauritian slave girls. The younger, Constance, was only nine years old; her companion, Elizabeth, was twelve.'

Edward Duyker, *Of the Star and the Key: Mauritius, Mauritians and Australia*, Sydney: Australian Mauritian Research Group, 1988, p. 37.

2. Between 1817 and 1840, forty-one ships sailed with more than one hundred convicts bound from Mauritius to New South Wales. These convicts comprised five categories: (1) Mauritian-born slaves or former slaves; (2) slaves or former slaves born in Mozambique or Madagascar; (3) Indian and Chinese indentured labourers; (4) British military prisoners convicted in Mauritius or transported from India; (5) escaped prisoners from Australia who were recaptured off ships which came into Mauritius.

Edward Duyker, *Of the Star and the Key: Mauritius, Mauritians and Australia*, Sydney: Australian Mauritian Research Group, 1988, p. 37.

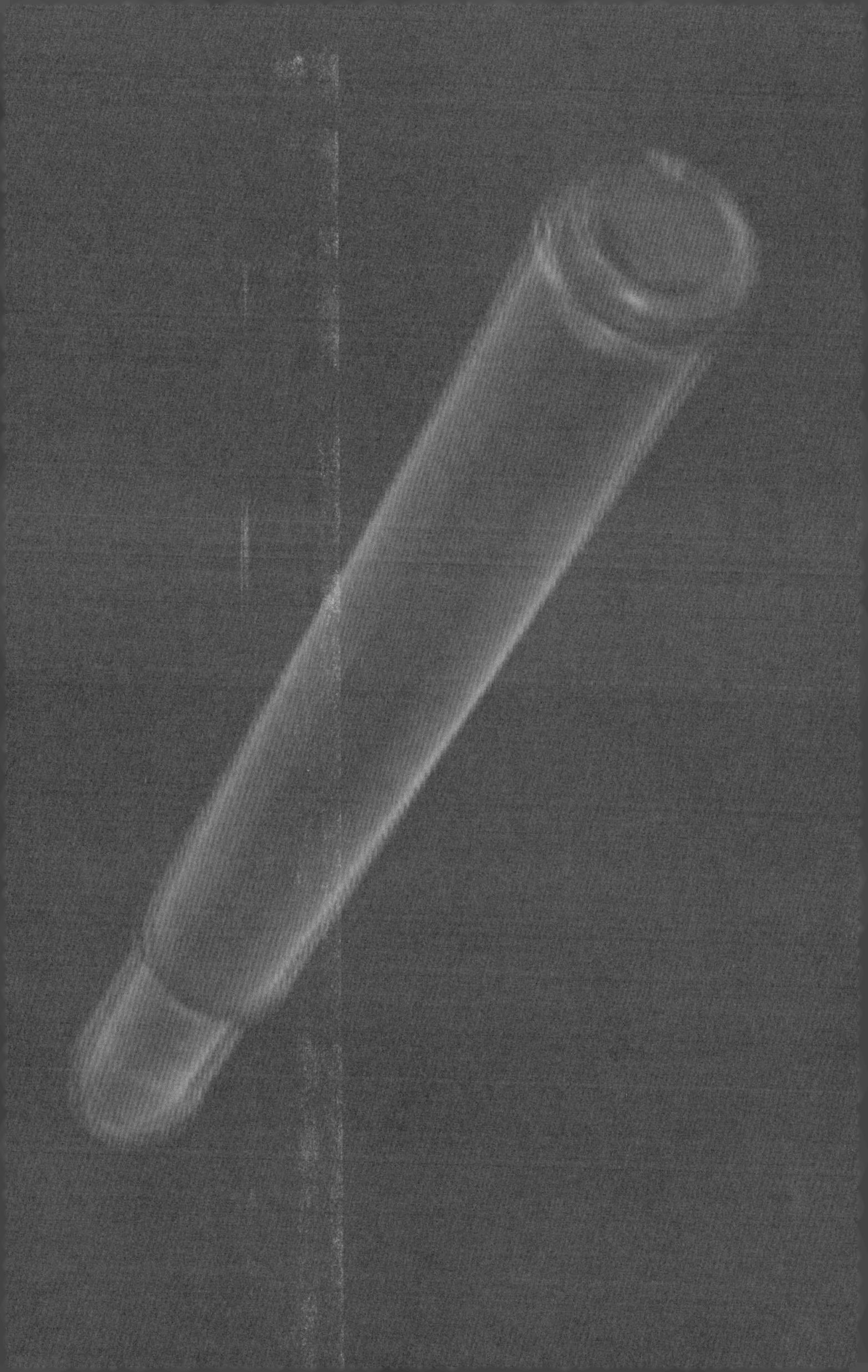

WHY ARE YOU WEEPING?

Trade Object: A mariner's telescope
Storyteller: An Aboriginal sailor

SAILOR: *I was on a ship over near Hawaii. We were sitting in the ocean there, for days and days. No wind. No fish. Nothing.*[1] *Every fella sitting down. What can we do? An American, he gives me his song.*

Why are you weeping, dear Mother
When I am on the sea?[2]
Is the same Providence, dear Mother,
Watching no more over me?
Think of the lessons you taught me
Even in my earliest years.
Practise their precepts, dear Mother,
And they will calm your fears.

Have I not seen you watching,
Oft from the stormlash'd shore?[3]
When the lightning dart was flashing,
Feared you the thunder's roar.
When for my father's danger,
I like a child have wept,
Did you not say that in heaven
Watch over his life was kept?

Be of good cheer, dear Mother,

Hope is my guiding star,
Be it yours, too, dear Mother,
When I am roaming far,
Oft will my home thoughts wander,
Over the stormy main,[4]
And in your dreams I'll whisper,
"Mother, we meet again"

Ah yes. Why are you weeping, dear mother?

Research Notes

Several Sydney Aborigines – Bon-del, Gnunga-Gnunga, Bungaree are the named and best-known examples – became skilled sailors who often shipped for long voyages. The Aboriginal mariners were researchers describing and analysing the incursive new cultures that the sailing ships were bringing to their country. They met all manner of people around the world and traded stories, songs and languages wherever they went. Bungaree was famous throughout the British empire. He was a cultural diplomat who relayed information and discursive protocols amongst several differentiated and wary communities. He spoke good Latin and was also awarded elocution prizes for English at the Sydney College.

See Ross Gibson, 'Ocean Settlement' in *Meanjin*, Vol. 53, No, 4, 1994; see also Jakelin Troy, *Australian Aboriginal Contact with the English Language in New South Wales: 1788 to 1845*, Canberra: A.N.U. Pacific Linguistic Series B 103, 1990.

'But if American whaleships were not important in the early Australian supply trade, American merchant ships were. The early supply trade ended with the outbreak of the Anglo-American war of 1812 and it did not revive until 1832. The port of Sydney was re-opened to American ships in 1831 and in the following year the *Tybee* of Salem formally re-opened the Australian-American trade. The American trading ships which visited Australia in increasing numbers after 1832 were mostly South Sea traders, vessels which specialised in supplying the United States Pacific whaling bases and collected in return cargoes of island products, wool and hides, and oil.'

L. G. Churchward, 'Notes on American Whaling Activities in Australian Waters 1800 - 1850', in *Historical Studies*, Nov. 1949, p. 62.

'Music and dancing were a part of life in wardroom and mess throughout the navy ... ... Some ships had bands of a sort, and privateers, for recruiting purposes, went out of their way to provide music.'

N.A.M. Rodger, *The Wooden World: An Anatomy of the Georgian Navy*, Annapolis, Maryland: Naval

Institute Press, 1986, p. 44.

1. 'Down dropt the breeze. the sails dropt down,
'Twas sad as sad could be;
And we did speak only to break
The silence of the sea!'

Samuel Taylor Coleridge, *The Rime of the Ancient Mariner*, 1798, Part II, ll. 107 - 110.

2. 'Seamen have always lived on the fringes of settled society. The Greeks hesitated whether to count them among the living or the dead.'

N.A.M. Rodger, *The Wooden World: An Anatomy of the Georgian Navy*, Annapolis, Maryland: Naval Institute Press, 1986, p. 15.

3. Fifty per cent of professional oceangoing men in the eighteenth century are estimated to have died of their work.

N.A.M. Rodger, *The Wooden World: An Anatomy of the Georgian Navy*, Annapolis, Maryland: Naval Institute Press, 1986, p. 53.

4. '[Shipmates and their fates] ...
HENRY FOULARTON, Midshipman.
Dead. Very religious, and remarkably neat in his dress; but at last drank very hard, and died regretting that a keg of gin (alongside of him) should see him out, which was really the case.

'ANDREW MACBRIDE, Schoolmaster.
Dead. Splendid abilities.
'GEO. GORDON, Assistant Surgeon.
Dead. George was not very orthodox.

'DUNCAN CAMPBELL, Assistant Surgeon.
Uncertain. Much the gentleman.

'JOHN MARSH, Assistant Surgeon.
Uncertain. Drank like a fish.'

James Anthony Gardner, *Above and Under Hatches: being Naval Recollections in shreds and patches with strange reflections*, written in 1836, edited by Christopher Lloyd, London: Batchworth, 1955, p. 70.

THE DREADFUL SHIPWRECK OF THE *HERO*

Trade Object: Fragments of dolls
Storyteller: A tavern singer performing a ballad for the assembled audience

SAILOR: *Draw near each tender Christian, assist my feeble hand,*
Until I relate this dreadful news, it's worth your while to stand,
Concerning those poor passengers from Liverpool sailed away,
On board the ship the Hero, *to them a woeful day.*

It was in the month of January, all in this present year,
We steered our course for Sydney, the weather it being fair,
When parting from old Erin's shore, we bid our friends goodbye,
We little thought when parting them it's in the deep we'd lie.

We were not far from Liverpool when heavy gales did blow,
For thirteen days our gallant ship was tossing to and fro;
But on the morning of the sixth, most dreadful for to hear,
Our vessel struck against a rock, which filled our hearts with fear.

It would make the hardest heart to grieve to hear the bitter cries,
Of the children and their mothers, the husbands and their wives
Crying 'now alas', 'what shall we do?', 'the ocean is our grave'.
It was our sad misfortune our home and friends to leave.

As for our noble captain, the truth for you I'll tell,
He treated us most tenderly and did his duty well,
Likewise our gallant seamen, their exertions proved in vain.
Our gallant ship in pieces went upon the raging main.

They then launched out their small boat upon the ocean wide,
While the children for their parents so bitterly they cried;
But to our great misfortune, as you may understand,
The boats they sank beneath the waves and could not reach the land.

Some of those poor passengers remained upon the deck,
And when our ship in pieces went, they floated on the wreck.
Some rocks then being convenient, it's on them they did creep,
While two hundred and twenty, young and old, were buried in the deep.

For two long days and two long nights, the truth I will explain,
We had to stop upon this rock, under wind and heavy rain,
Thinking on the friends we lost, for to increase our grief,
When the ship the Rose *of Boston bore down to our relief.*

So now to conclude these feeling lines, I have no more to say.
We lost two hundred and twenty folk in a deep and dismal sea;
Holy Mary, pray for them that now lie in the deep.
May the Lord have mercy on their souls, and grant their friends relief.

See William Alexander Barratt, *English Folk-Songs collected, arranged and provided with symphonies and accompaniments for the pianoforte*, Darby: Norwood, 1973.

Research Notes

Ocean ballads of parting and loss circulated in great numbers, on broadside sheets, in taverns and cabins, all over the world during the eighteenth and nineteenth centuries. Here is one more example, from tens of thousands of possible choices.

Now I am bound for a foreign land,
All against my inclination.
Yes, I must leave my native home,
Which fills me with vexation.
And as I'm bound for Sydney's coast,
Nature, she still does bind me
To think of her I do adore –
The girl I left behind me.

My foes have sent me far away
For fear I'd wed my darling,
The bonny lass I love so well,
How mild she is, how charming.
When crossing those unfriendly waves,
I thought the tears would blind me,
Full many a heavy sigh I gave
For the girl I left behind me.

Unto the land of perfidy,
Our vessel she is sailing,
Methinks I never can be free,
Now that I've parted from my Ellen.
For though I'm going far away,
Nature still does bind me,
To think on her I do adore –
The girl I left behind me.

Oh cruel fates who banished me
And left me broken hearted!

Sweet Ellen dear, though far from me,
Our hearts shall never be parted!
Though now I'm in Port Jackson's gaol,
Constant still you'll find me.
Oh no! I never will forget
The girl I left behind me.

Was I possessed of all the gold
That lies on the African strand,
I'd give it all now to behold
My own dear native land.
Near Tyneside town of ebbing tides,
Once more, my friends, you'll find me –
It's there my Ellen does reside –
The girl I left behind me.

Had I full wealth and so much gold
To me 'twould be no measure.
The bonny lass that I adore
Is worth much more than treasure.
Farewell you bonny lasses all.
From her you shall not bind me.
My thoughts go to my native home,
To the girl I left behind me.

This folk tradition of songwriting was turned to commercial bounty in 1865 by Henry Work Clay, a Chicago printer who penned *The Ship that Never Returned* and was amazed to watch it become beloved all over the world. Even today, it is a popular favourite in English pubs:

On a bright summer morning
When the waves were rippling
In the soft and sighing breeze,
A ship set sail with a precious burden
To a port beyond the seas.
There, beyond farewells and loving gestures

and the hearts all left to burn.
But they sailed away with a smile and a blessing
On the ship that never returned.

That never returned, that never returned,
And its fate is still unlearned.
They sailed away with a smile and a blessing
On the ship that never returned.

'Oh,' said the pale-faced boy to his loving mother,
'Oh, let me cross the wide, wide sea.
For they tells me that in a foreign country
There is health and wealth for me.'
So he kissed his mother with a fond affection,
The lad for whom her heart always yearned.
And he sailed away with his mother's blessing
On the ship that never returned.

That never returned, that never returned,
And his fate is still unlearned.
He sailed away with his mother's blessing
On the ship that never returned.

'Only one more trip,' said the gallant sailor
As he kissed his fond young wife.
'Only one more bag of the golden treasure
And we'll settle down for life.
Oh we will leave this place for a little cottage
And enjoy the wealth we've earned.'
But from that day to this, she's been watching and waiting
For the ship that never returned.

That never returned, that never returned,
And its fate is still unlearned.
And from that day to this she's been watching and waiting
For the ship that never returned.

See Fred Jordan, *Songs of a Shropshire Farm Worker*, London: Topic Records, 1966, 12T150.

THE COAST OF PERU

Trade Object: Barrel of flour
Storyteller: A young whalehunting sailor

SAILOR: *Come all you young fellows that's bound after sperm,*
Come all you bold seamen that have rounded the Horn,
Our Captain has told us and we hope he says true
That there's plenty of sperm whales off the coast of Peru.

Well we've rounded the Horn and we're now off Peru,
And we're all of one mind to endeavour to do,
Our boats they're all ready and the masthead is manned,
Our rigging's rolled lightly, boys, and the signal's all planned.

It was early one morning, we heard the brave shout,
As the man in the lookout cries out 'there she spout',
'Where aweigh?' says our Captain, 'And where do she lay?'
'Two points to our lee bow, scarce a mile away!'

Well, it's call up all hands me boys, and be of good cheer!
Put your tubs in your boats and have your bowlines all clear,
Tow away on them ropes now, jump in, my brave crew,
Row away now and after her, try the best you can do.

Well the waist boat run down and of course got the start.
'Lay on,' says the harpooner, 'For I am hell for the long dart.
Now bend on them oars, me boys, make your Boat fly.
But there's one thing we dread – oh, keep clear of her eye!'

Well the first iron struck and the whale she went down,
But as she came up again the Captain he bent on.
And the next harpoon stuck and the line sped away.
The one thing that whale done, she gave us fair play.

Well she raced and she sounded, she twisted and spin,
But we brought her alongside, and we got our lance in,
Which caused her to spew forth and the blood for to spout,
And in ten minutes time, me boys, she'd rolled both fins out.

So we hauled her alongside with many a shout,
And we soon cut her in and began to try out.
Now the blubber is rendered and likewise dealt down,
And it's better to us, me boys, than five hundred pound.

Now we're bound into Sydney in our manly power,
Where a man buys a whorehouse for a barrel of flour.
We'll spend all our money on them lewd girls ashore,
And when it's all gone, me boys, we'll go whaling for more.

This is a traditional sailor's song about the Southeast Pacific whaling grounds, adapted from a version which can be heard on the *Layers* recording by Chris Foster, Topic Records 12TS329 (1977).

Research Notes

'See with what entire freedom the whaleman takes his handful of lamps – often but old bottles and vials, though – to the copper cooler at the try-works, and replenishes them there, as mugs of ale at a vat. He burns, too, the purest of oil, in its unmanufactured, and, therefore, unvitiated state; a fluid unknown to solar, lunar, or astral contrivances ashore. It is sweet as early grass butter in April. He goes and hunts for his oil, so as to be sure of its freshness and genuineness, even as the traveller on the prairie hunts up his own supper of game.'

Herman Melville, *Moby-Dick*, first published in 1851, Chapter XCVII.

'Where should the child of England look but to the sea! The sea is our birthright and inheritance. Nature herself seems to point out to us our proper path and our real interests, by keeping us constantly in sight of the ocean. She presents an impenetrable barrier to further inroads into the interior of the Country by an impassable morass; whilst she allures us to the almost interminable length of Coast, swarming with whales, and intersected by gulphs, creeks and harbours, without equals in the world, absolutely inviting us to make use of them.'

Anon., 'Australian Sperm Whale Fishery', in *The Australian Quarterly Journal of Theology, Literature and Science*, Number 1 (1828), pp. 87 - 88.

TRADE LISTS

At random intervals, the walls of the Bond Store murmur lists of items that were traded through Sydney during the first fifty years of the colony.

Now landed and on sale in our stores ... 240 Double Gloucester cheeses. Same number of Cheddar. 70 bladders of Irish hogs lard. 60 real bath chops, superior to the best hams. One hundred boxes of sperm and wax candles. 50 barrels of superior Scotch oatmeal. One hundred barrels of fine Yarmouth herrings. Orange, lemon and citron peel. 40 casks of percussion gunpowder in one-pound cannisters. 30 bags of subtle pimiento. Black pepper and assorted pickles. 15 barrels of Jamaica ginger. 50 boxes of muscatell raisins. 20 tons of pure London soap. 95 hundredweight of Epsom salts. Five tons of salted whiting. 100 barrels of Portuguese peas. 500 caddies of best soochong tea. 20-pound jars of best quality snuff. 100 bags of dark Manila coffee. One thousand mats of best Mauritius sugar. Spices of every variety. Mustard, cigars, pearl ash and soda. Rotton stone, dip candles, wick and lamp cotton. York hams, tapioca, arrowroot, castor oil. Brimstone, beeswax, tartar cream, black lead. Lucifer matches, chocolate wafers. Pencils, vermicelli and macaroni. Scented soap, twine and split peas.

Now landed and on sale in our stores .... Big-bowled pipes, made to order for the New Zealand trade. Blankets of sizes suitable for New Zealand. Jujube and fruit lozenges. Copal and mastic varnish. Quicksilver. Corrosive sublimate. Oil of vitriol. Blue stone. Sarsparilla. Seidlitz powder in neat mahogany cases. Acidulated drops. Trotter's tooth powder. Oil of tar and quinine. Amputating cases. Dissecting tools and cupping instruments. Enema apparatus. Stomach pumps. Catheter, syringes, silver probes. Preserved hare in twelve-pound tins. Same of grouse and Cotswold partridge. Yorkshire bacon in prime order. Tahitian salt pork. Irish salt pork. Fruit-flavoured snuff of all kinds.

Now landed and on sale in our stores ... Flour and sugar, cheap by virtue of being impregnated with tar. Maltese window glass. Chinese preserves and American crackers. Acidulated lemon-flavoured lozenges. Irish linen. Three Indian stallions. Spears and clubs from New Zealand. Also mats and shells. Lacquerware in the Japanese style. Maps of New South Wales in sheets, rollers and cases. Hogsheads of Cape Madeira wine. Youths and boys drab hats from London. Parasols, elastic garters and black silk stockings. Double-barrelled fowling pieces with powder and shot. Fresh supplies of perfumery from America. Anti-corrosive paint. North American reindeer tongues, hams and cheese. Prime anchovies and essence of same. Gentlemen's shaving and toilet glasses. Stationery and cutlery of all kinds. Irish brooms and brushes of every description.

Now landed and on sale in our stores ... Morocco slate books. Draft boards and men. Chessmen. Splendid steel pens. Mathematical instruments. Parallel rules. Gunter scales. Pocket compasses. Alphabets in boxes. China tiles. Razor strops and paste. China ink in powder. Patent pencil pointers. Memorandum books, ledgers and journals. Comic conversation cards. Flowers of loveliness. Forget-me-nots. Friendship's Offering. Book of gems. Original poems in two volumes. Nursery rhymes. Nautical Almanack for coming year.

Domestic Cookery, by a much-esteemed lady. Ure's Chemical Dictionary. Lord Byron's works complete in one volume. Cooper's patent pickle jars, in four sizes. Tortoiseshell ladies' combs from the East Indies. White pullets and hens in fair condition. Ribbons from Naples, all colours. Fine Hamburg quills. Desiccated south seas coconut. Marseilla and Portuguese wines priced cheap.

Now landed and on sale in our stores ... Red precipitate of mercury. Barbadoes aloes. Iodine. Honey. Strychnine. Morphia. Potash. Oil of lemon. Essence of bergamotte. Quinine. Kreosote. Opium. Archil. Alum. Coriander seeds. Flower of sulphur. Oil of peppermint. Henry brand magnesia. Ching's worm lozenges. Powell's pills. Hunt's pills. Cockle's pills. Leeming's ointment. Congreve's elixir. A quantity of leaf tobacco. Drums, trumpets and tin whistles. Bats, balls and stumps. Skipping ropes and whips. Walking sticks. Humming tops. Dolls and their houses. Shuttlecocks. Magic fish, ships and geese. Fishing rods, hooks and lines. Dissected maps designed as puzzles. Bengal twine. Cork butter. New Zealand red potato. 30 loads of blue-gum plank. Brussels carpeting and chimney armaments. Dutch toys of wood. American whaling gear of all kinds. Brazil tobaccos. Pianofortes in good order. Pincushions and thimbles. India rubber balls. Rocking horses. Doll's heads, shoes and arms. Banker's bill books. Brewer's thermometers. Chinese ivory parasol rings. Ornaments from East Indies. Pink saucers. Office penknives. Waggons, carts and wheelbarrows, for the amusement of children.

THE BOND STORE EXHIBITION CREDITS

Crew

Project Co-ordinator / Senior Curator	Peter Emmett
Writer / Director	Ross Gibson
Technical Design	Gary Warner
Producer	Vincent Sheehan
Director of Photography	Jackie Farkas
Sculptor / Set Designer	Marcus Skipper
Display Fitout	Sebastian Giner, Phillip Ward
Costume Designers	Milvia Harder, Edie Kurzer
Make-up / Hair Stylist	Annabelle Barton
Sound Recordist	Dennis Archer
Camera Assistant	Anna Craney
Production Assistant	Carla Drago
Still Photographs	Ian Hobb, Carla Drago Jackie Farkas, Vincent Sheehan
Digital Video Effects	Alistair Ferguson
Songs arranged and recorded by	John Willsteed
Post Production Sound Design	Andrew Plain
Sound Mixer	David White
Post Production Sound Facility	Counterpoint Sound
Technical Design and Installation	Tim Gruchy
Control Programming	John White
Object Research	Beth Hise, Caroline Mackaness Jo Anne Pomfrett, Joy Thompson

Actors

Sentry Spiel	Russell Cheek
Our Canvas-sack Man	Paul Moore
A Man Always in Check	Anna Volska
In the Eyes of an Albatross	Keith Robinson
These are all New Spectacles	Paul Goddard
Bon-del Tells Me	Ghandi McIntyre
Can You be this Unlucky?	Drayton Morley
Consider Yourself	Paul Sonkila
Do Not Chatter in Useless Argot	Geoff Minard
Let Us Pray	Jaclyn Hewett
The Aire of Malbrooke	Bill O'Toole
Like a Knife on a Fine China Plate	Clarence Dany
Mad for the Use of Body	Julie Prasad
Mr Macleay's Bunyip	Don Reid
No Swine in Sydney's Bushland	Robert Carlton
Nothing is Wasted	Maureen Green
On this Day	Gillian Jones
Look Upon My Works	Cormac Costello
Sing of God's Garrison	Roy Billings
Smoke Smells like God	Mic Gruchy
Something So Bad	Rachel McGuigan
Tell Him Things	Lillian Crombie
Who Controls the Rum Store	Colleen Cross
The Coast of New Zealand	Michelle Andringa
The Cure	Ralph Cotterill
The Secret Language of Teeth	Noah Taylor
The Touch of Gentleness	Sally Cahill

Two Distant Planets	Lech Mackiewicz
Walking our Streets	Joe Laveta
Wealth is what you set your Mind to	Gillian Hyde
This Colour Red	Steve Rodgers
Who Can Sing with Me Now?	Sara Zwangobani
Why are You Weeping?	Kevin Smith
Shipwreck of the Hero	Kathy Wemyss
The Coast of Peru	Roger Norris

Specimens in 'Holding Cage'

From the Macleay Museum, University of Sydney:
Green Turtle, Emu, Pelican, Black Swan, Red-tailed Black Cockatoo, Eastern Grey Kangaroo, Giant Clam, Conch Shell, PNG Crocodile, Deer Skeleton, Indian Silver-leaf Monkey, Madagascar Brown Lemur, Baby Elephant Skull.

From the Australian Museum:
African Zulu Shield, Chinese Storage Jar, Fijian Kava Bowl, South Pacific Wicker Shield and Spear and Club, Solomon Islands Paddle, PNG Spears.

From Vaucluse House, Historic Houses Trust:
Mirror, Oak Chest, Escutcheon, Ceramic Footstools, Wire Birdcage, Marble Column, Gilt Frame, Barrels.

Images in Story Backgrounds

Solitude - Tristan de Acunha - Watching the Horizon, Augustus Earle, 1824. Rex Nan Kivell Collection, National Library of Australia.

Tristan de Acunha, Augustus Earle,1824. Rex Nan Kivell Collection, National Library of Australia.

Rafting Blubber at Tristan de Acunha, Augustus Earle, 1824. Rex Nan Kivell Collection, National Library of Australia.

A North Easter, Tristan de Acunha, Augustus Earle, 1824. Rex Nan Kivell Collection, National Library of Australia.

Summit of Tristan de Acunha, A Man killing an Albatross, Augustus Earle, 1824. Rex Nan Kivell Collection, National Library of Australia.

Natives of New South Wales in the Streets of Sydney, Augustus Earle, 1830. Rex Nan Kivell Collection, National Library of Australia.

Flinching a Young Sea Elephant, Tristan de Acunha, Augustus Earle, 1824. Rex Nan Kivell Collection, National Library of Australia.

Portrait of Bungaree, a native of New South Wales, Augustus Earle, ca 1826. Rex Nan Kivell Collection, National Library of Australia.

St George Sealing off the Island of Jan Mayen, artist unknown, 1846. Rex Nan Kivell Collection, National Library of Australia.

Shipwreck, Kent, artist unknown, c1890. National Library of Australia.

An Episode on the ship St Malo crossing the line, Theodore Kirby, 1854. Rex Nan Kivell Collection, National Library of Australia.

The Sperm Whale, Owen Stanley, 1846 - 1849. Mitchell Library, State Library of New South Wales.

Becalmed Near the Line - Hands to Bathe, Owen Stanley, 1846.

Mitchell Library, State Library of New South Wales.
Amateur Whaling, Oswald Brierly, 1847. Australian National Maritime Museum.

South sea Whalers Boiling Blubber, J. Greenaway after O. Brierly, 1876. Australian National Maritime Museum.

Whaling, Lady's Bay, Tasmania, William Duke, c1840. Queen Victoria Museum and Art Gallery, Launceston.

Raja Sarabhojie of Tanjore, artist unknown, c1825. Victoria and Albert Museum, London.

Idol Juggernaut on his Car taken during Rath Jatra, artist unknown, c1822. Victoria and Albert Museum, London.

Four Women Selling Food-grains, Vegetables and Fruit, Shiva Dayal Lal, c1850. Victoria and Albert Museum, London.

Patient from the Canton Hospital, Lam ua, c1840. Yale University Medical Library.

Matthew Flinders, explorer, Will Longstaff. National Trust of South Australia.

Floral Still Life, Tinua, c1855. Peabody Essex Museum, Salem, Massachusetts.

Sydney Cove, 1793, Fernando Brambila, 1793. British Library.

The North Cape of New Zealand, Joel Samual Polack. Alexander Turnbull Library, Wellington.

Weighing and Purchasing Tea, artist unknown, c1820. Peabody Essex Museum, Salem.

Boats Attacking Whales, W. J. Linton. Alexander Turnbull Library, Wellington.

Archival Film in Story Backgrounds

ABC TV
Storms, Edge of the Cold, Man the Killer Man the Keeper, Ocean Wanderers, The Dominant Male, The Dolphin Hunters

Australian Board of Missions
Martyr's Harvest

Australian Museum
Apanji Village

Ballarat School of Mines
Wonders of the Sea

Film Australia
Antarctic Voyage 1956, Pearlers of the Coral Sea, Solomon Islands, The Islanders, Whaling at Norfolk Island

Cinesound / Film World Research
Whaling Season Booms

National Film and Sound Archive
Scene in Singapore - Home Movie, Mystery Island

Methodist Mission Society of Australia
The Transformed Isle

University of Sydney Archive
Elkin and Briggs footage - PNG

National Film and Sound Archive
Coorab on the Island of Ghosts, For the Term of His Natural Life, 90 Degrees South, Cannibals and Christians of the South Seas, Devil's Playground (1928), Home of the Blizzard, In New Guinea Wilds, Jungle Woman, Nature's Little Jokes, Pearls and Savages, Siege of the South, Lumieres Bros., Queensland footage, Gladstone Home Movies, Fiji, Crossroads of the South Pacific, The Sugar Industry in Cairns, The First Underwater Film

LIST OF BOOK ILLUSTRATIONS

Page x & xi: *Shipwreck, Kent* (detail), artist unknown, c1890. National Library of Australia.

Page 1: MIDDLE *Natives of New South Wales drinking "Bull"*, W.H. Fernyhough. Mitchell Library, State Library of New South Wales. LEFT *For the Term of His Natural Life* (film still). National Film and Sound Archives (NFSA).

Page 2: TOP *Bust of an Aboriginal woman*, Nicolas-Martin Petit, 1802. Lesueur Collection, Museum d'Histoire Naturalle, Le Havre, France. BOTTOM *For the Term of His Natural Life* (film still). NFSA.

Page 3: MIDDLE *Native Dancing*, Lieutenant Philip Gidley King, c1789-93. Mitchell Library, State Library of New South Wales. LEFT *Devils Playground* (film still). NFSA.

Page 4: TOP LEFT *For the Term of His Natural Life* (film still). NFSA. BOTTOM LEFT *Flinching a Young Sea Elephant, Tristan de Acunha*, Augustus Earle, 1824. Rex Nan Kivell Collection, National Library of Australia. RIGHT *Australian Aborigine carrying spear and fish*, T.R. (Richard) Browne, c1820. Mitchell Library, State Library of New South Wales.

Page 5: LEFT *For the Term of His Natural Life* (film still). NFSA. RIGHT *Devils Playground* (film still). NFSA.

Page 6 & 7: *Shipwreck, Kent* (detail), artist unknown, c1890. National Library of Australia.

Page 10: Robert Cheek in *Sentry Spiel*.

Page 11: MIDDLE *Porcelain shop* (detail), c1820-30. Peabody Essex Museum, Salem, Massachusetts. BOTTOM *Four Women Selling Food-grains, Vegetables and Fruit*, Shiva Dayal Lal, c1850. Victoria and Albert Museum, London.

Page 12: *Weighing and Purchasing Tea*, artist unknown, c1820. Peabody Essex Museum, Salem.

Page 15: *Ceremonial club*, copy based on a *Basalt patu* belonging to Kawerau tribe of Auckland. Collection of Auckland Museum.

Page 16: Paul Moore in *Our Canvas-sack Man.*

Page 17: TOP *Moon*, Gibson Home Movies. G.I.A. Collection. BOTTOM *Coorab in the Island of Ghosts* (film still). NFSA.

Page 18: RIGHT *Crying Over The Bones of a Dead Chief. New Zealand*, Augustus Earle, 1828. Rex Nan Kivell Collection, National Library of Australia. LEFT *Pearls and Savages* (film still). NFSA.

Page 23 & 24: Anna Volska in *A Man Always in Check. Ebony and pine chess pieces.* Rouse Hill House collection.

Page 25: TOP *Matthew Flinders, explorer*, Will Longstaff. National Trust of South Australia. BOTTOM *Gladstone Home Movies* (film still). NFSA.

Page 26: *Floral Still Life*, Tinua, c1855. Peabody Essex Museum, Salem.

Page 30: Keith Robinson in *In the Eyes of an Albatross. Mahagony watercolour paintbox*, Rowney and Forster, c1820. Elizabeth Bay House collection.

Page 31: TOP *Portait of Bungaree, a native of New South Wales, with Fort Macquarie, Sydney Harbour, in background*, Augustus Earle, c1826. Rex Nan Kivell Collection, National Library of Australia. CENTRE *Siege of the South* (film still). NFSA. BOTTOM LEFT *Solitude - Tristan de Acunha - Watching the Horizon*, Augustus Earle, 1824. Rex

Nan Kivell Collection, National Library of Australia. BOTTOM RIGHT *A man killing albatross Tristan D'Acunha*, Augustus Earle, 1824. Rex Nan Kivell Collection, National Library of Australia.

Page 32: TOP *Siege of the South* (film still). NFSA. BOTTOM *A man killing albatross Tristan D'Acunha*, Augustus Earle, 1824. Rex Nan Kivell Collection, National Library of Australia.

Page 36: Paul Goddard in *These are all New Spectacles.*

Page 37: *Patient from the Canton Hospital*, Lam ua, c1840. Yale University Medical Library.

Page 41: Oil lamp. *Elizabeth Farm collection.*

Page 42: Ghandi McIntyre in *Bon-del Tells Me.*

Page 43: TOP *Fishing, Plate 2*, John Heaviside Clark, 'Field Sports of the Native Inhabitants of the New South Wales', London, 1813. Courtesy Cornstalk Bookshop, Sydney. BOTTOM *Pearls and Savages* (film still). NFSA.

Page 44: TOP & BOTTOM *Pearls and Savages* (film still). NFSA.

Page 45: *Home of the Blizzard* (film still). NFSA.

Page 49: *Wrought iron fence*, 1820s. Graveyard at St Matthews, Windsor.

Page 50: Drayton Morley in *Can You be this Unlucky?*

Page 51: *For the Term of His Natural Life* (film still). NFSA.

Page 52: *Home of the Blizzard* (film still). NFSA.

Page 55: *Ivory handmirror, hallmarked silver mount.* Private collection.

Page 56: Paul Sonkila in *Consider Yourself.*

Page 57: TOP *90 Degrees South* (film still). NFSA. BOTTOM RIGHT *Jungle Woman* (film still). NFSA. BOTTOM LEFT *For the Term of His Natural Life* (film still). NFSA.

Page 60: Geoff Minard in *Do Not Chatter in Useless Argot. Poetic works of Sir Walter Scott*, 1803. Vaucluse House collection.

Page 61: RIGHT *Pearls and Savages* (film still). NFSA. LEFT *Siege of the South* (film still). NFSA.

Page 65: *The Book of Common Prayer*. Vaucluse House collection.

Page 66: Jaclyn Hewett in *Let Us Pray.*

Page 67: *The Sugar Industry in Cairns* (film still). NFSA.

Page 72: Bill O'Toole in *The Aire of Malbroooke.*

Page 73: TOP *Briggs Footage - PNG* (film still). University of Sydney Archive. BOTTOM RIGHT *Pearls and Savages* (film still). NFSA. BOTTOM LEFT *Cannibals and Christians of the South Seas* (film still). NFSA.

Page 74 & 75: *The Aire of Malbrooke*, sheet music.

Page 79: *Silver cutlery.* Vaucluse House collection.

Page 80: Clarence Dany in *Like a Knife on a Fine China Plate.*

Page 81: RIGHT *Briggs Footage - PNG* (film still). University of Sydney Archive. LEFT *Crossing the Line*, Owen Stanley, 1837-1843. Mitchell Library, State Library of New South Wales.

Page 82: *For the Term of His Natural Life* (film still). NFSA.

Page 85: Copy of *Copper nails*, based on originals from the wreck of the *Sirius*. Courtesy of National Maritime Museum.

Page 86: Julie Prasad in *Mad for the Use of Body.*

Page 87: *Gna.na.gna.na*, Port Jackson Painter. The Natural History Museum, London.

Page 91: *Mounted skin from the Hawkesbury River* Cyclops *or* Bunyip, 1841. Macleay Museum, University of Sydney.

Page 92: Don Ried in *Mr Macleay's Bunyip.*

Page 93: TOP *Skull, Hawkesbury River* Cyclops *or* Bunyip, 1841. Macleay Museum, University of Sydney. BOTTOM *Stock Footage* (film still). Film Australia.

Page 96: Robert Carlton in *No Swine in Sydney's Bushland.*

Page 97: *Cannibals and Christians of the South Seas* (film still). NFSA.

Page 98: *Fire*, Gibson Home Movies. G.I.A. Collection.

Page 99: *Cannibals and Christians of the South Seas* (film still). NFSA.

Page 101: *Barrel.* Vaucluse House collection.

Page 102: Maureen Green in *Nothing is Wasted.*

Page 103: *Natives of New South Wales drinking "Bull"*, W.H. Fernyhough. Mitchell Library, State Library of New South Wales.

Page 105: *Sydney Gazette*, Saturday, March 5, 1803. Mitchell Library, State Library of New South Wales.

Page 106: Gillian Jones in *On This Day. Cup and saucer,* Worcester, c1835 *and silver teapot,* 1840s. Elizabeth Bay House collection.

Page 109: *Poetic works of Sir Walter Scott,* 1803. Vaucluse House collection.

Page 110: Cormac Costello in *Look Upon My Works.*

Page 111: *VIEW of the EAST SIDE of SIDNEY COVE, PORT JACKSON; from the ANCHORAGE. The GOVERNOURS HOUSE bearing S.bE.1/2E. & the FLAG STAFF S.EbE.1/4E,* George Raper, c1789. The Natural History Museum, London.

Page 115: *Original pulpit,* 1828. St James Church collection.

Page 116: Roy Billings in *Sing of God's Garrison.*

Page 117: TOP *Cannibals and Christians of the South Seas* (film still). NFSA. BOTTOM *Martyr's Harvest* (film still). Australian Board of Misssions.

Page 122: Mic Gruchy in *Smoke Smells like God.*

Page 123: Mic Gruchy in *Smoke Smells like God* (detail).

Page 124: TOP *Cannibals and Christians of the South Seas* (film still). NFSA. BOTTOM The Sugar Industry in Cairns (film still). NFSA.

Page 125: *Devils Playground* (film still). NFSA.

Page 130: Rachel McGuigan in *Something So Bad.*

Page 131: TOP *Cannibals and Christians of the South Seas* (film still). NFSA. BOTTOM *First Underwater Film* (film still). NFSA.

Page 135: *Writing equipment.* Rouse Hill House collection. *Ink pot.* Sydney Cove Authority Archaeology Collection.

Page 136: Lillian Crombie in *Tell Him Things.*

Page 137: *Tell Him Things* (video still).

Page 141: *Bottle.* First Government House Archaeology collection.

Page 142: Colleen Cross in *Who Controls the Rum Store? Crystal fluted drinking goblets, crystal decanter and silver tray.* Elizabeth Bay House collection.

Page 145: *Chinese umbrella.* Private collection.

Page 146: Michelle Andringa in *The Coast of New Zealand.*

Page 147: TOP *Amateur Whaling,* Oswald Brierly, 1847. Australian National Maritime Museum. BOTTOM *Boats Attacking Whales,* W.J. Linton. Alexander Turnbull Library, Wellington.

Page 148: TOP *The Sperm Whale,* Owen Stanley, 1846-1849. Mitchell Library, State Library of New South Wales. BOTTOM *Whales Amusing Themselves to the Great Astonishment of Mr. Brown and the Second Gallies Crew - Torres Straits,* 1848-49, Owen Stanley. Mitchell Library, State Library of New South Wales.

Page 152: Ralph Cotterill in *The Cure.*

Page 153: *Porcelain shop* (detail), c1820-30. Peabody Essex Museum, Salem.

Page 154: TOP & BOTTOM *Siege of the South* (film still). NFSA.

Page 155: TOP *St George Sealing off the Island of Jan Mayen*, artist unknown, 1846. Rex Nan Kivell Collection, National Library of Australia. MIDDLE *Siege of the South* (film still). NFSA. BOTTOM *Cannibals and Christians of the South Seas* (film still). NFSA.

Page 160: Noah Taylor in *The Secret Language of Teeth. Hammock.* Hyde Park Barracks Museum.

Page 161: *For the Term of His Natural Life* (film still). NFSA.

Page 162: *For the Term of His Natural Life* (film still). NFSA.

Page 167: *Pin cushion, cotton-reel holder and selected sewing items from the Anna Blaxland workbox.* Vaucluse House collection.

Page 168: Sally Cahill in *The Touch of Tenderness. Bonnet*, early 1800s. Elizabeth Farm collection.

Page 169: TOP & BOTTOM *Devils Playground* (film still). NFSA.

Page 171: Copies based on large wooden club from the Port Jackson area. N.M. Miklukho-Maklay Institute, Leningrad collection.

Page 172: Lech Mackiewicz in *Two Distant Planets.*

Page 179: Copy of *walking stick* based on the popular clenched fist motif of the early 19th century.

Page 180: Joe Laveta in *Walking in our Streets this Morning.*

Page 181: TOP & BOTTOM *Cannibals and Christians of the South Seas* (film still). NFSA.

Page 182: TOP *First Underwater Film* (film still). NFSA. BOTTOM *Devils Playground* (film still). NFSA.

Page 185: *Earthenware jar.* Vaucluse House collection.

Page 186: Gillian Hyde in *Wealth is what you set your Mind to.*

Page 187: TOP & BOTTOM *Panorama of Sydney*, after Major James Taylor, 1821, detail from panel 2, *The Town of Sydney in New South Wales.* Museum of Sydney on the site of first Government House.

Page 188: *Panorama of Sydney*, after Major James Taylor, 1821, detail from panel 1, *The Entrance of Port Jackson.* Museum of Sydney on the site of first Government House.

Page 193: *Panorama of Sydney*, after Major James Taylor, 1821, detail from panel 1, *The Entrance of Port Jackson.* Museum of Sydney on the site of first Government House.

Page 196: Sara Zwangobani in *Who Can Sing with Me Now?*

Page 197: *90 Degrees South* (film still). NFSA.

Page 198: *Climbing trees*, John Heaviside Clark, 'Field Sports of the Native Inhabitants of the New South Wales', London, 1813. Courtesy Cornstalk Bookshop, Sydney.

Page 201: *Spyglass.* Mitchell Library, State Library of New South Wales.

Page 202: Kevin Smith in *Why are you Weeping?*

Page 203: TOP *Becalmed Near the Line - Hands to Bathe*, Owen Stanley, 1846. Mitchell Library, State Library of New South Wales. BOTTOM RIGHT *For the Term of His Natural Life* (film still). NFSA. BOTTOM LEFT *Pearls and Savages* (film still). NFSA.

Page 207: *Ceramic toys.* Sydney Cove Authority Archaeology collection.

Page 208: Kathy Wemyss in *Shipwreck of the Hero.*

Page 209: TOP *90 Degrees South* (film still). NFSA. BOTTOM *Home of the Blizzard* (film still). NFSA.

Page 210: *First Underwater Film* (film still). NFSA. BACKGROUND *Dreadful shipwreck of the 'Hero'*, sheetmusic.

Page 215: *Barrel.* Vaucluse House collection.

Page 216: Roger Norris in *The Coast of Peru.*

Page 217: TOP *The North Cape of New Zealand,* Joel Samuel Polack. Alexander Turnbull Library, Wellington. BOTTOM *Shipwreck, Kent* (detail), artist unknown, c1890. National Library of Australia.

Page 218: LEFT *Boats Attacking Whales,* W.J. Linton. Alexander Turnbull Library, Wellington. RIGHT *Whales Amusing Themselves to the Great Astonishment of Mr. Brown and the Second Gallies Crew - Torres Straits,* 1848-49, Owen Stanley. Mitchell Library, State Library of New South Wales.

Opened on 20 May 1995, this new museum on this historic site is a meeting place to discover anew this place they called Sydney. It is built on the ruins of Governor Phillip's 1788 house, exposed by archaeologists in the 1980s. MOS explores this beautiful and bizarre world of colonial Sydney through objects, pictures and new digital-media technologies.

Access and Parking

MOS is located on the corner of Phillip and Bridge Streets. Parking is available in the Governor Phillip car park, entry from Young or Phillip Streets. Discount parking is available to visitors on weekends. Stop 2 on the Explorer bus route. Disabled and pram access to all areas.

Exhibitions

The Focus Gallery presents a program of exciting temporary exhibitions.

Public Programs

A wide range of events to enrich the core exhibits – seminars, live performances, dance, theatre, focus talks.

Education Programs

MOS offers a number of specially designed education programs for K-12. Discuss a day package visiting other Trust properties.

MOS Shop

For books, postcards, craft, jewellery, commissioned works and gifts, all with a Sydney flavour.

MOS Venue Hire

MOS is available for functions – breakfasts, dinners, seminars, launches.

MOS Cafe

MOS Cafe is located on First Government House Place and is open daily 7am to 10pm, weekends 10am to 8pm. Telephone 02 9241 3636.

Museum of Sydney *on the site of first Government House* is open to the public daily, 10am to 5pm, except Christmas Day and Good Friday.
Telephone 02 9251 5988 for more information

The Historic Houses Trust of NSW is a statutory authority, created by the NSW Government, which manages important historic sites in NSW for the education and enjoyment of the public. The Museum of Sydney *on the site of first Government House* represents a bold new endeavour for the Trust: an exciting contemporary project that draws on innovative resources, themes, ideas and displays.

Properties of the Historic Houses Trust include:
Elizabeth Bay House, Elizabeth Bay
Elizabeth Farm, Parramatta
Government House, Sydney
Hyde Park Barracks Museum, Sydney
Justice and Police Museum, Sydney
Lyndhurst, Glebe
Meroogal, Nowra
Museum of Sydney *on the site of first Government House*, Sydney
Rose Seidler House, Wahroonga
Rouse Hill House, Rouse Hill
Susannah Place, The Rocks
Vaucluse House, Vaucluse

Enquiries 02 9692 8366

All information is correct at time of printing, but may be subject to change

The Bond Store Tales

Editor: Ross Gibson
Sub Editor: Mireille Juchau
Publications Coordinator: Rebecca Haagsma
Image Clearance: Michelle Andringa
Design & Production: Karen McKenzie

Printed in Australia by RT Kelly Pty Limited, Sydney
Paper supplied by Raleigh Paper Co Pty Ltd, Sydney
dustjacket - Novatech Gloss
cover - Parilux Dull White
endpapers - Gilclear Medium
text - Poseidon Vellum